LEARNING AND SKILLS

Longman Essential Psychology
Series editor: Andrew M. Colman

LEARNING AND SKILLS

EDITED BY

Nicholas J. Mackintosh
and
Andrew M. Colman

LONGMAN
London and New York

Longman Group Limited
Longman House, Burnt Mill
Harlow, Essex CM20 2JE, England
and Associated Companies throughout the world.

*Published in the United States of America
by Longman Publishing, New York*

© 1994 Routledge
This edition © 1995 Longman Group Limited
Compilation © 1995 Andrew Colman

This edition first published 1995

ISBN 0 582 27809 0 PPR

British Library Cataloguing-in-Publication Data
A catalogue record for this book is available from the British Library.

Library of Congress Cataloging-in-Publication Data
A catalogue record for this book is available from the Library of Congress.

Typeset by 25 in 10/12pt Times
Printed and bound by Bookcraft (Bath) Ltd

CONTENTS

NOTES ON EDITORS AND CONTRIBUTORS

JOHN ANNETT is Professor of Psychology at Warwick University. He took his doctorate at Oxford in 1959, has taught at the Universities of Sheffield, Aberdeen and Hull and was Professor of Psychology at the Open University. His current research interest is in motor imagery and other 'cognitive' aspects of motor skills. He is chairman of the Motor Skills Research Exchange and Psychology Editor of the Journal of Sport Sciences. Among his publications are *Feedback and Human Behaviour* (1969) and *Training in Transferable Skills* (1989).

MICHAEL ARGYLE is Emeritus Reader in Social Psychology at Oxford University, a fellow of Wolfson College, Oxford and Emeritus Professor at Oxford Brookes University. He has been Chairman of the Social Psychology section of the British Psychological Society and Visiting Professor at various universities in the United States, Canada, Australia, and elsewhere. He is the author of *The Psychology of Interpersonal Behaviour* (4th edn, 1983), *Bodily Communication* (2nd edn, 1988), *The Social Psychology of Work* (2nd edn, 1989), *The Social Psychology of Everyday Life* (1992), *Psychology and Social Class* and other books and papers.

DONALD M. BAER is the Roy A. Roberts Distinguished Professor of Human Development and Family Life, and of Psychology, at the University of Kansas, Lawrence. He took his doctorate at the University of Chicago in 1957, and taught at the University of Washington in Seattle before beginning his current employment with the University of Kansas in 1965. He has also taught briefly at universities in Canada, Australia, Japan, and Brazil. He has published many articles on behaviour analysis and its application, especially to problems of children, and on its use as a theoretical framework for the study of child development. He has served as president of the international Association for Behavior Analysis. His most persistent research and conceptual target has been the problem of securing appropriately generalized results from clinical interventions into behaviour problems.

ANDREW M. COLMAN is Reader in Psychology at the University of Leicester, having previously taught at Rhodes and Cape Town Universities in South Africa. He is the founder and former editor of the journal *Current Psychology* and Chief Examiner for the British Psychological Society's Qualifying Examination. His books include *Facts, Fallacies and Frauds in Psychology* (1987), *What is Psychology? The Inside Story* (2nd edn, 1988), and *Game Theory and its Applications in the Social and Biological Sciences* (2nd edn, 1995).

K. ANDERS ERICSSON is the Dr Edward Conradi Eminent Scholar Chair in Psychology at the Florida State University, Tallahassee. He is the co-author (with Herbert A. Simon) of *Protocol Analysis: Verbal Reports as Data* (1984), which appeared in a second revised edition in 1993. He is the co-editor (with Jacqui Smith) of *Toward a General Theory of Expertise: Prospects and Limits* (1991).

NICHOLAS J. MACKINTOSH is Professor of Experimental Psychology at the University of Cambridge and a fellow of King's College, Cambridge. He has previously taught at the University of Oxford, Dalhousie University, Nova Scotia, and the University of Sussex, and, more briefly, at the University of Hawaii, the University of Pennsylvania, and at Bryn Mawr College. He has written several books on animal learning, including *The Psychology of Animal Learning* (1974) and *Conditioning and Associative Learning* (1983), and is currently writing one on human intelligence.

WILLIAM L. OLIVER received his doctorate at the University of Colorado and has done postgraduate research at the Learning, Research, and Development Center in Pittsburgh, Pennsylvania. He is currently Assistant Professor of Psychology at Florida State University. He is pursuing research on skill acquisition and computer models of learning and memory.

SERIES EDITOR'S PREFACE

The *Longman Essential Psychology* series comprises twelve concise and inexpensive paperback volumes covering all of the major topics studied in undergraduate psychology degree courses. The series is intended chiefly for students of psychology and other subjects with psychology components, including medicine, nursing, sociology, social work, and education. Each volume contains five or six accessibly written chapters by acknowledged authorities in their fields, and each chapter includes a list of references and a small number of recommendations for further reading.

Most of the material was prepared originally for the Routledge *Companion Encyclopedia of Psychology* but with a view to later paperback subdivision – the contributors were asked to keep future textbook readers at the front of their minds. Additional material has been added for the paperback series: new co-editors have been recruited for nine of the volumes that deal with highly specialized topics, and each volume has a new introduction, a glossary of technical terms including a number of entries written specially for this edition, and a comprehensive new index.

I am grateful to my literary agents Sheila Watson and Amanda Little for clearing a path through difficult terrain towards the publication of this series, to Sarah Caro of Longman for her patient and efficient preparation of the series, to Brian Parkinson, David Stretch, and Susan Dye for useful advice and comments, and to Carolyn Preston for helping with the compilation of the glossaries.

ANDREW M. COLMAN

INTRODUCTION

Nicholas J. Mackintosh
University of Cambridge, England

Andrew M. Colman
University of Leicester, England

Dictionaries usually define learning as the acquisition of knowledge or information and skills. So we may learn Latin grammar, the capital cities of Europe, the kings and queens of England, or how to tie our shoelaces and ride a bicycle. Psychologists, however, define learning both more narrowly and more widely than this. The acquisition of knowledge is usually studied by psychologists under the rubric of research on memory. Hermann Ebbinghaus, the first psychologist to study how people (usually himself, for he acted as his own main subject) learned lists of words and "nonsense syllables" published the results of his research in a book he called *Über das Gedächtnis*, which means literally "on memory" (Ebbinghaus, 1913), and the nomenclature has stuck. Thus most of this research is described in Alan Baddeley's chapter on memory in the volume entitled *Cognitive Psychology* in this series (French & Colman, 1995).

But psychologists also define learning more widely than the acquisition of information or skills. Whenever any change in our behaviour may be attributed to particular past experiences, they will be likely to explain that change in terms of learning. At one time or another, they have talked as though we must learn to see, how to understand spoken language, and speak in our turn, to tell the truth and to lie, to recognise our friends and relatives, or the difference between the taste of claret and of burgundy. Our beliefs about the world, our attitudes, prejudices and stereotypes, our phobias and obsessions, all are the product of learning.

The psychological study of learning acquired this broad scope at the time of the behaviourist revolution announced and led by John B. Watson (1913, 1924). Watson's main target was introspectionism, already discredited by the inability of different psychologists to agree with one another about the most basic content of their introspections. The goal of behaviourism was to turn psychology into an objective science by ensuring that its subject matter was confined to observable facts about human (and animal) behaviour. But Watson also had other targets in sight. One of his aims was to banish the concept of instinct from psychology, to disallow explanations of our behaviour that appealed to the herd instinct or the solitary instinct, the suicidal instinct or the survival instinct, the English instinct to make Sunday gloomy, or the crusaders' instinct to liberate the Christian subjects, of the Sultan.

For Watson, these were all fictions. We are born with no more than a handful of basic reflexes as our innate endowment. For the rest, we are a product of learning and conditioning:

> There are then for us no instincts – we no longer need the term in psychology. Everything we have been in the habit of calling an "instinct" today is a result largely of training – belongs to man's *learned behavior*. As a corollary from this we draw the conclusion that there is no such thing as an inheritance of *capacity*, *talent*, *temperament*, *mental constitution* and *characteristics*. These things again depend on training that goes on mainly in the cradle. (Watson, 1924, p. 94)

Today, behaviourism is commonly denounced as an unfortunate aberration in the history of psychology. No doubt, Watson's environmentalism was as extreme as his insistence on banishing mental life or his reduction of thinking to sub-vocal speech. But just as there was much that was salutary in behaviourism's rejection of introspectionism, so there has been much of lasting benefit from psychology's attempts to analyse the role of experience in shaping our attitudes and temperament, and the ways in which past learning affects our current behaviour.

As soon as we define learning more widely than the acquisition of knowledge and skills, there becomes less reason to confine our study of the learning process to people. If there are general principles of learning common to the huge variety of circumstances in which learning is manifest, perhaps those general principles will be most readily discovered and analysed by studying learning by simpler animals in simpler situations. Thus was born, in the 1930s and 1940s in the United States, the age of the grand learning theories of Guthrie, Hull, Skinner, and Tolman. This was a time when a man like Tolman, the most "cognitive" of these theorists and thus, one might have supposed, the most sensitive to some of the complexities of our own cognitive processes, could write:

> I believe that everything important in psychology (except such matters as the building of a super-ego, that is everything save such matters as involve society and words) can be investigated in essence through the continued experimental and

theoretical analysis of the determiners of rat behavior at a choice point in a maze. Herein I believe I agree with Professor Hull. (Tolman, 1938, p. 34)

As is often the way, lasting contributions to science come less from grandiose theory and more from careful and patient experimentation aimed at discovering lower-level principles. Thus the study of animal learning and conditioning today, as Nicholas J. Mackintosh's opening, chapter in this volume makes clear, owes less to these learning theorists than to the work of two earlier experimenters, Ivan Pavlov and Edward Thorndike, who undertook the first systematic laboratory experiments on classical (or Pavlovian) and instrumental (or operant) conditioning respectively. The term *conditioning* and the verb *to condition* are back formations from a mistranslation of Pavlov's Russian terrninology. He distinguished between stimuli that unconditionally elicited a reflex response (as dry food unconditionally or automatically elicits salivation from a hungry dog), and other stimuli (his flashing lights, buzzers, or metronomes) that would do so only conditionally – that is, if they had previously signalled the delivery of food. The terms were translated as unconditioned and conditioned instead of unconditional and conditional respectively.

The laboratory study of learning and conditioning in animals, for many years regarded as a cornerstone of experimental psychology, eventually came under attack from two opposite directions, on the one hand from cognitive psychologists who rightly questioned Tolman's dictum quoted above, and on the other from ethologists studying animal behaviour under more natural conditions, who (also rightly) questioned Watson's extreme environmentalism. However controversial may be the notion of genetic determination of differences between people in temperament, personality, or intelligence, no one could seriously doubt that the behaviour of different species of animals differs because of genetic differences between them. According to one extreme version of this argument, indeed, the search for general principles of learning is futile: what a particular animal learns, and how it learns it, is a consequence of its past evolutionary history and current adaptive specialization.

The argument surely contains an element of truth, but it should not be exaggerated. General principles of learning uncovered in the laboratory have been shown to be readily applicable to the behaviour of animals going about their daily activities – foraging for food and discovering what is good to eat and what is bad, identifying other individuals of their own species, and avoiding predators (for example, Shettleworth, 1994). But what of the application to human behaviour? Again, no one would suppose that the principles of learning uncovered in simple conditioning experiments with rats, rabbits, and pigeons will tell us everything we want to know about how people solve problems, how they reason by analogy, test hypotheses, or discover and apply general rules. Nevertheless, recent studies of human learning have begun to reveal unsuspected simplicity in some cases. Unintentional, incidental, or "implicit" learning, the detection of the frequency with which certain events occur, and statistical regularities and contingencies between them, can all be analysed in terms of associative learning theories very similar to those popular with psychologists studying animal conditioning (Shanks, 1994).

Moreover, the attempt to apply certain basic principles of conditioning to everyday human behaviour has by now a long and often successful history. Although Skinner's analysis of instrumental or operant conditioning owes a lot to Thorndike's earlier concept of trial and error learning, whereby unsuccessful actions dropped out and successful ones were retained, Skinner's major original contribution to psychology was perhaps to see the power and generality of this principle of reinforcement by consequences. As Donald M. Baer's chapter 2 in this volume makes clear, the application of this basic principle of instrumental conditioning (plus one or two others) has provided a powerful way of understanding much of our everyday behaviour, and possibly of changing that behaviour when it is maladaptive or undesirable. Skinner's prescriptions for human society have been denounced by those who see them as an attack on human freedom and dignity, and terms such as behaviour modification, behavioural engineering, or control can easily sound alarm bells. Skinner's retort, which has often been ignored, harks back to Watson: we are what we are as a consequence of past learning, of a myriad of past, unplanned contingencies of reinforcement acting to shape us in ways of which we are often unaware. It is past learning that has made us what we are: if we do not like this outcome, an understanding of these principles of learning may help us to change.

For more information on the psychology of learning than can be contained in this slim volume see Mackintosh (1994); and for a good introduction to animal, especially primate, intelligence, which is not covered here at all, see Byrne (1995).

The study of complex, organized patterns of behaviour acquired through training and practice is traditionally carried out in a field of research devoted specifically to skills, which draws heavily on theories and findings from the psychology of learning. Research into skills can be traced at least as far back as the 1820s, when the German astronomer Friedrich W. Bessel began to study the accuracy of difficult astronomical observations requiring judgements of duration. In the latter half of the nineteenth century and the early decades of the twentieth investigations continued into how people learn Morse code, typing, and other skills, and research in this field gained considerable momentum during the Second World War with the development of radar, advanced military aircraft, and sophisticated weapon systems, which presented human operators with difficult problems of learning and performance. More recently, especially since the 1970s, research on skills has been further stimulated by the rise of sports psychology and increased concern about skilled aspects of social interaction.

Cognitive skills such as mathematics or chess, which are discussed by K. Anders Ericsson and William L. Oliver in chapter 3 of this volume, are usually distinguished from perceptual skills such as radar monitoring, from motor skills such as juggling, and from social skills such as non-verbal communication. According to this conventional though somewhat arbitrary and conjectural classification, cognitive skills are those that depend mainly on intellectual or information processing abilities rather than on complex or difficult feats of perception, motor coordination, or social interaction. Ericsson and Oliver outline the acquisition of simple and everyday cognitive skills before discussing, at some length, research into high-level cognitive skills or expertise. Readers with a special interest in this area might find the book by Esther Thelen (1994), which presents a different: developmental approach to cognitive and other skills, additionally useful.

In chapter 4, John Annett reviews the major theoretical and empirical contributions to the study of motor skills. At a time when behaviourism was influential, skill acquisition was interpreted as a process of forming stimulus-response links (for example, Thorndike, 1932). A problem with this approach was its difficulty in representing the structured complexity of some skills, and this led to the development of a theoretical interpretation of skills as hierarchically structured motor programs – organized patterns of movements stored in memory – subject to feedback control. Annett explains these theories and the associated research evidence, and also discusses the acquisition and retention of motor skills and the issue of transfer of training – the positive and negative effects of a learnt skill on the performance of a different, related activity.

The last chapter, by Michael Argyle, is on social skills, which are simply those necessary for competent verbal and non-verbal social interaction. Argyle describes techniques for assessing social behaviour, the components of social skills, and methods of training people to be more socially skilled. For a fuller discussion of social skills, see Hargie, Saunders and Dickson (1994).

In addition to the references cited in this introduction, every chapter of this book contains recommendations for further reading for the benefit of readers who wish to delve more deeply into the psychology of learning and skills.

REFERENCES

Byrne, R. (1995). *The thinking ape*. Oxford: Oxford University Press.

Ebbinghaus, H. (1913). *Memory: A contribution to experimental psychology*. Translated by H. Ruyer & C. E. Bussenius, New York: Teachers College, Columbia University. (Original German work published 1885.)

French, C. C., & Colman, A. M. (1995). *Cognitive psychology*. London and New York: Longman Group Limited, ch. 1.

Hargie, O., Saunders, C., & Dickson, D. (1994). *Social skills in interpersonal communication* (3rd edn). London: Routledge.

Mackintosh, N. J. (ed.) (1994). *Animal learning and cognition: Handbook of perception and cognition* (2nd edn, vol. 9). San Diego, CA: Academic Press.

Shanks, D. R. (1994). Human associative learning. In N. J. Mackintosh (ed.), *Animal learning and cognition: Handbook of perception and cognition* (2nd edn, vol. 9 pp. 335–74). San Diego, CA: Academic Press.

Shettleworth, S. J. (1994). Biological approaches to the study of learning. In N. J. Mackintosh (ed.), *Animal learning and cognition: Handbook of perception and cognition* (2nd edn, vol. 9 pp. 185–219). San Diego, California: Academic Press.

Thelen, E. (1994). *A dynamic systems approach to the development of cognition and action*. Cambridge, MA: MIT Press.

Thorndike, E. L. (1932). *The fundamentals of learning*. New York: Teachers College, Columbia University.

Tolman, E. C. (1938). The determiners of behavior at a choice point. *Psychological Review*, *45*, 1–41.

Watson, J. B. (1913). Psychology as the behaviorist views it. *Psychological Review*, *20*, 158–77.

Watson, J. B. (1924) *Behaviorism*, New York: Norton.

1

CLASSICAL AND OPERANT CONDITIONING

Nicholas J. Mackintosh
University of Cambridge, England

The laws of association	**Associative learning in humans**
Pavlovian and instrumental	**Further reading**
conditioning	**References**
Hierarchical associations	

There was a time when standard textbooks of experimental psychology afforded a central place to the study of conditioning and learning in animals. The learning theories of the American psychologists Clark Hull, Edward Tolman, Edwin Guthrie, and B. F. Skinner were regarded, and not only by their authors, as among psychology's most fundamental theoretical contributions to the understanding of human behaviour. Few psychologists would now grant learning theory such an exalted position. Indeed, the study of conditioning is more often derided as artificial or, an even worse fate, ignored as boring and irrelevant. Both the earlier adulation and the later denigration are surely unjustified. The study of conditioning in animals is not the key to all psychology, but it is certainly more interesting and probably more important than its detractors have supposed.

The scientific study of conditioning dates back to the beginning of the twentieth century, to the experiments of Ivan Pavlov (1849–1936) in Russia and Edward Thorndike (1874–1949) in the United States, working in quite different traditions and in total ignorance of one another. Pavlov developed the general procedures for studying classical (or Pavlovian) conditioning, invented a terminology to describe it that is still in use, and advanced an account of what was happening in his experiments, many elements of which are still widely accepted. In the course of his work on the digestive system of the dog, Pavlov had found that salivary secretion was elicited, not only by placing food in the dog's mouth but also by the sight and smell of food, and even by the sight and sound of the technician who usually provided that food. Anyone who has prepared dinner for their pet dog will not be totally amazed by Pavlov's discovery. In a dozen different ways, that include excited panting and jumping and also profuse salivation, dogs show that they recognize the familiar precursors of their daily meal. For Pavlov, at first, these "psychic secretions" merely interfered with the planned study of the digestive system; but he then saw that he had a tool for the objective study of something even more interesting – how animals learn.

Pavlov's experiments on conditioning employed a standard simple procedure (Pavlov, 1927). A hungry dog is restrained on a stand and every few minutes is given some dry meat powder, whose occurrence is signalled by an arbitrary stimulus, such as the illumination of a lamp or the ticking of a metronome. The food itself elicits copious salivation, and after a few trials the ticking of the metronome, which regularly precedes the delivery of the food, will also elicit salivation. In Pavlov's terminology the food is an unconditional stimulus (US), because it invariably (unconditionally) elicits salivation, which is termed an unconditional response (UR). The ticking of the metronome is a conditional stimulus (CS) because its ability to elicit salivation (now a conditional response (CR) when it occurs to the CS alone) is conditional on a particular set of experiences. The occurrence of the CR to the CS is termed a conditional reflex which is reinforced by the presentation of the US (food) – so that the US itself is often termed a reinforcer. In the absence of food the repeated presentation of the CS alone will result in the gradual disappearance or extinction of its CR.

Thorndike's typical experiment involved placing a cat inside a "puzzle box" from which the animal could escape and obtain food only by pressing a panel, operating a catch, or pulling on a loop of string (Thorndike, 1911). Thorndike measured the speed with which the cats gained their release from the box on successive trials, observing that the animals would initially behave aimlessly or even frantically, stumbling on the correct response or responses purely by chance, but would eventually execute these responses efficiently and economically within a few seconds of being placed in the box. Thorndike's procedures were greatly refined by Skinner (1938), who delivered food to the animal inside the box via an automatic delivery device, and could thus record the probability or rate at which animals performed the designated response over long periods of time without having to handle them. Skinner also adopted some of Pavlov's terminology, referring to his procedure as one of operant (or instrumental) conditioning, to the food reward as a reinforcer of conditioning, and to the decline of responding, when the reward was no longer available, as extinction. In Skinner's original experiments, the animals were laboratory rats who were required to depress a small lever protruding

2

from one wall of the box in order to obtain a small pellet of food. Subsequently the "Skinner box" was adapted for pigeons, who were required to peck at a small illuminated disk on one wall of the box in order to obtain some grain.

The traditional theory of conditioning was built round these simple experiments, where learning was evidenced by the animal acquiring a new response. After conditioning the dog now salivates to the ticking of the metronome, the rat presses the lever, the pigeon pecks the illuminated disk. Conditioning then seemed to be a matter of the strengthening of a new conditional reflex, or, in Thorndike's analysis, the formation of a new connection or bond between a stimulus and a response. But as soon as one departs from this one rather limited experimental paradigm, this description immediately seems less appropriate: not all learning seems to be a matter of the acquisition of new responses. The rat in the Skinner box who learns to press a lever if rewarded with a pellet of food for doing so, will learn even more rapidly to refrain from pressing the lever if each lever press results in the delivery of an electric shock as well as a pellet of food (Mackintosh, 1983, p. 124). What *new* response has been acquired, or stimulus–response connection strengthened, as a result of this experience? Similarly, many instances of Pavlovian conditioning are only with difficulty described as the establishment of new reflexes. Thirsty rats will avidly drink a sweet-tasting sucrose solution, but if its ingestion is followed by an injection of lithium chloride, which makes the animal mildly ill, they will condition an aversion to the sucrose solution, refusing to touch it the next day (Revusky & Garcia, 1970). What is the new stimulus–response connection that has been formed? The measure of conditioning is a decline in responding (drinking of sucrose); it seems more plausibly described as a revaluation of the initial attractive solution, so that it is now regarded as aversive.

That the traditional stimulus–response account of conditioning is seriously misleading is confirmed by a slightly more elaborate experiment, illustrated in Table 1 (see Dickinson, 1989; Rescorla, 1991). In the first stage of the experiment, a rat is trained to press a lever in a Skinner box or operant chamber to obtain sucrose pellets. In the second stage, the rat is given cause to revalue the sucrose pellets: after eating some in another environment the rat receives an injection of lithium chloride which conditions an aversion to

Table 1   Design for reinforcer revaluation experiment

Stage 1	*Stage 2*	*Stage 3*
Rat trained to press lever for sucrose pellets	Rat given sucrose pellets to eat followed by lithium injection	Rat given opportunity to press lever (no sucrose pellets available)

sucrose pellets. The test phase simply asks whether the rat will press the lever again when replaced in the operant chamber. Common sense suggests that the rat should not, and common sense is right: the rat does refrain from pressing the lever (significantly more than various control groups). But how is this to be explained by the traditional stimulus–response account? According to this analysis, what the rat learned in the first place was to press the lever whenever it came into view. The function of the sucrose pellet was simply to strengthen a new connection between sight of lever and response of pressing. Once this new stimulus–response connection has been formed, no change in the value of the sucrose will have any further bearing on it: the rat would stop pressing the lever only if given the opportunity to learn something new about the consequences of so doing – that lever pressing was no longer rewarded, for example, or was actually punished. It seemed reasonable to suppose that the rat should refrain from pressing a lever which has previously produced sucrose pellets that are now no longer valued, because we implicitly took it for granted that what the rat had learned, was first, that lever pressing produces sucrose pellets, and second, that sucrose pellets are no longer valuable; we then assume that the rat can put these two pieces of information together. But this is not how learning is represented by stimulus–response theory.

Similar revaluation effects occur in simple Pavlovian conditioning experiments. If a CS is paired with sucrose pellets and comes to elicit an appropriate appetitive CR, this CR will be abolished by subsequently conditioning an aversion to the sucrose pellets (Holland & Straub, 1979). Here we must assume that the original conditioning established an association between some central representations of the CS and the sucrose pellets rather than simply strengthening a new reflex between CS and CR. The implication is that conditioning is not reducible to the strengthening of new reflexes or stimulus–response connections by the automatic action of a process of reinforcement. It is more profitably viewed as the process by which animals detect and learn about the relationship between events in their environment, be those events stimuli, responses, or reinforcers, and adjust their behaviour accordingly.

THE LAWS OF ASSOCIATION

Viewed from this perspective, conditioning experiments arrange contingencies between events, and animals associate those events. In a typical Pavlovian experiment, the experimenter arranges that food will be presented whenever the metronome starts ticking, never at other times. The dog associates the ticking of the metronome with the delivery of food, and the salivary CR that develops is an index of the formation of this association. If the experimenter continued to present food following the metronome alone, but on other trials turned on a flashing light at the same time as the

4

metronome and delivered no food, the dog would presumably learn that the light signalled the absence of the food and the formation of such an 'inhibitory' association would be evident from the dog's tendency not to salivate whenever the light accompanied the metronome – and from the fact that the light would equally inhibit salivation when presented in conjunction with a second independently trained positive CS (Rescorla, 1969).

In a typical operant experiment the experimenter arranges that the delivery of food is dependent on the animal's execution of a particular response – the rat pressing a lever, the pigeon pecking an illuminated disk. By parity of reasoning, we might suppose that this contingency between response and food results in the formation of an association between the two, and that the change in behaviour we observe – an increase in the probability of lever pressing or disk pecking – is an index of this associative change. Of course, if the reinforcer contingent on lever pressing had been an aversive event such as shock, the same association between response and reinforcer would have resulted in a decline in the probability of responding.

The next question to be addressed is what are the conditions under which associations between CSs and reinforcers or responses and reinforcers are formed. Classical associationist theory of British empiricist philosophy, which long antedates the laboratory study of conditioning, usually assumed a very small number of laws of association, of which the most prominent was that of temporal contiguity. Two events will be associated if and only if they occur in strict temporal contiguity. It turns out that, for conditioning at least, this is seriously misleading. Temporal contiguity is certainly important, for the rat that will learn to press a lever when a pellet of food is delivered immediately after each lever press will learn more slowly when a delay of even a few seconds is imposed between lever pressing and food. But even so, learning will occur with intervals of 30–60 seconds (Dickinson, Watt, & Griffiths, 1992); in other conditioning preparations, mostly Pavlovian, successful conditioning can occur with delays of a minute or more between presentation of the CS and the delivery of the reinforcer. The most famous example of this is the food aversion conditioning procedure referred to earlier (Revusky & Garcia, 1970). A rat that consumes a novel-flavoured substance at one time can condition an aversion to that substance, even if the interval between consumption and illness is several hours. This finding has led some investigators to suppose that food aversion conditioning represents a unique adaptive specialization of learning, which may not obey the same laws as other more arbitrary forms of conditioning (Rozin & Kalat, 1971; Seligman, 1970). As Revusky (1971) has noted, however, there are numerous parallels between food aversion conditioning and other more conventional paradigms: for example, although conditioning occurs over longer intervals than those usually effective in other paradigms, it still varies inversely with the length of the interval separating ingestion and sickness; an aversion produced by making a rat sick after ingesting one substance does not generalize completely

5

:to other flavours (Mackintosh, 1983, p. 203). This can mean only that the aversion is a consequence of associating the specific substance ingested with the subsequent illness.

But it is clear that strict temporal contiguity between response or CS and reinforcer is not absolutely necessary for successful conditioning. More important than this, however, is the demonstration that it is not the *absolute* temporal relationship between, say, a CS and the reinforcer that determines how readily conditioning will occur, but the *relative* temporal proximity of the two. In pigeons, brief illumination of a disk of light before the delivery of food will result in conditioning manifest as pecking the illuminated disk (a phenomenon sometimes termed "autoshaping"). Such conditioning occurs more readily with a reasonably short interval between CS and food. But what is more important is the length of this interval relative to the interval between successive trials; where this inter-trial interval is short, say 24 seconds, conditioning will occur much more rapidly if the interval between onset of CS and food is also short — 4 seconds rather than 8 or 16 seconds. But when the interval between trials is long, the interval between CS and US can also be

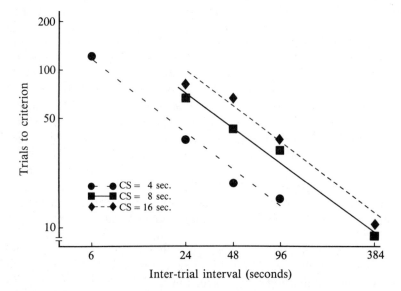

Figure 1 Speed of conditioning (measured by the number of trials required to reach a predetermined level of responding) as a function of the duration of each trial and of the interval between trials. Both axes are plotted on log coordinates. Speed of conditioning was inversely related to trial duration, but within each trial duration (points joined by regression lines) trials to criterion decreased as the intertrial interval increased. But note that, for example, the three groups with trial and inter-trial intervals of 4 and 24 seconds, 8 and 48 seconds, and 16 and 96 seconds all conditioned at the same rate

Source: Gibbon, Baldock, Locurto, Gold, and Terrace, 1977

lengthened without detracting from successful conditioning (Gibbon, Baldock, Locurto, Gold, & Terrace, 1977). Indeed, as Figure 1 shows, Gibbon and colleagues found that across a range of absolute values, a constant ratio between these two intervals resulted in a constant level of conditioning.

Relative temporal proximity is not the only newly established law of conditioning that raises problems for the classical associationist analysis. So does the phenomenon of relative validity. Successful conditioning will occur even if the CS is not always followed by a reinforcer, or if the response is not consistently reinforced. Indeed, Skinner's best-known contribution to the study of operant conditioning was the description and analysis of a variety of schedules of intermittent reinforcement (Ferster & Skinner, 1957), when a rat's lever presses or a pigeon's pecks are reinforced only after a certain passage of time (interval schedules), or after a certain number of responses have been performed (ratio schedules). Such schedules can typically generate rapid and persistent responding. But there is now good evidence that a CS which will elicit reliable CRs even if only intermittently followed by a reinforcer, will cease to do so if the reinforcer also occurs in the absence of the CS. In the limiting case when the probability of the reinforcer is the same in the absence of the CS as it is in its present, one typically finds no evidence of conditioning at all. The classic experiments to demonstrate this were undertaken by Rescorla (1968), studying conditioned suppression in rats, a procedure in which a CS is paired with the delivery of a brief shock while a hungry rat is pressing a lever for occasional food reinforcement. Conditioning to the CS is measured by the extent to which it suppresses the rate at which the rat presses the lever. As Figure 2 shows, the magnitude of conditioned suppression in Rescorla's experiments was not only a direct function of the probability of shock in the presence of the CS, but also an inverse function of the probability of shock in the absence of the CS. When these two probabilities were equal the CS elicited no suppression at all.

The implication of these studies is that conditioning depends on the extent to which a CS signals a *change* in the rate or probability of a reinforcer. One way of understanding this is to turn to a slightly different set of experiments, those on blocking. In experiments on conditioned suppression in rats, Kamin (1969) found that animals exposed to a compound CS, consisting of a light and a noise signalling shock, would normally condition to both elements of the compound. But prior conditioning to one element of the compound alone would attenuate or block conditioning to the other element. The design and results of one of Kamin's experiments are shown in Table 2. It is clear that blocking of conditioning to the light occurred because the light–noise compound signalled the same reinforcer as that signalled by the noise alone; as is shown in the third group in Table 2, when an additional unpredicted shock was programmed after each compound trial, substantial conditioning accrued to the light. Subsequent experiments have confirmed the conclusion

7

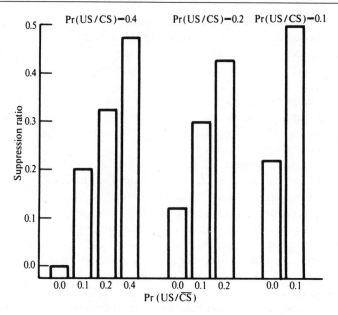

Figure 2 Conditioned suppression in rats as a function of the probability of shock in the presence and absence of the CS. A suppression ratio of 0.50 indicates that the CS did not suppress responding (i.e., no conditioning); one of 0.00 indicates complete suppression (i.e., strong conditioning). The probability of shock is calculated over 2-minute intervals (i.e., the duration of the CS); thus the first four groups received an average of 0.4 shocks per CS and between 0 and 0.4 shocks per 2-minute interval in the absence of the CS

Source: Rescorla, 1968

that blocking is a consequence of the added stimulus predicting no change in reinforcement from that signalled by the pretrained stimulus · alone (Dickinson & Mackintosh, 1979; Rescorla & Wagner, 1972).

Rescorla and Wagner (1972) proposed a formal model of conditioning which explains most of these results in a simple and elegant way. They

Table 2 Design and results of Kamin's blocking experiment

Group	Stage 1	Stage 2	Test results
Blocked	Noise → shock	Noise + light → shock	No conditioning to light
Control	—	Noise + light → shock	Conditioning to light
Surprise	Noise → weak shock	Noise + light → strong shock	Conditioning to light

suggest that conditioning depends on the discrepancy between obtained and expected reinforcement. In Kamin's (1969) blocking experiment, the shock is fully predicted by the noise by the end of Stage 1. There was thus no discrepancy between obtained and expected shock when the light was added to the noise, and therefore no conditioning to the light. To explain Rescorla's own experiments on relative validity, and the Gibbon et al. (1977) experiment on the temporal spacing of trials, we need only add the assumption that animals associate the occurrence of a reinforcer not only with a discrete CS, but also with the entire experimental context in which conditioning trials occur. Successful conditioning to the CS thus depends on its signalling an increase in the probability of the reinforcer over that already predicted or expected on the basis of the context alone. One final virtue of Rescorla and Wagner's model is its ability to integrate both excitatory and inhibitory conditioning. As noted above, inhibitory conditioning occurs if CS 1 is paired with a reinforcer but when CS 2 is added to CS 1 no reinforcer occurs: according to Rescorla and Wagner (1972) CS 2 now becomes a conditioned inhibitor because it signals the absence of an otherwise expected reinforcer, that is, a negative discrepancy between obtained and expected reinforcement.

PAVLOVIAN AND INSTRUMENTAL CONDITIONING

Essentially all the laws of association described above for the case of Pavlovian conditioning can also be demonstrated in instrumental or operant conditioning. Operant conditioning occurs only when a response is followed by an otherwise unexpected change in reinforcement: no conditioning will occur when the probability of the reinforcer is the same whether or not the rat presses the lever, and instrumental conditioning will be blocked if the occurrence of the reinforcer is better predicted by any other, discrete signal than by the occurrence of the response (Mackintosh & Dickinson, 1979). Conversely, if the reinforcer is better predicted by the response than by the signal, the response will block conditioning to the signal (Garrud, Goodall, & Mackintosh, 1981). The implication is that the same laws govern the formation of associations between related events regardless of whether those events are stimuli or responses.

But it is equally important to understand the distinction between classical and operant conditioning. The operational distinction, first clearly enunciated by the Polish psychologists Miller and Konorski (1928) and by Skinner (1938), is that in a Pavlovian experiment the experimenter arranges a relationship between a stimulus and a reinforcer regardless of the subject's behaviour; but in an instrumental experiment, the experimenter arranges a relationship between the subject's behaviour and the reinforcer. The argument so far has assumed that animals can associate these related events, and that such associations are formed in accordance with the same laws. The distinction between Pavlovian or classical and operant conditioning concerns the ways in which these associations are translated into changes in behaviour, and arise because reinforcers are events with two distinct properties. They are USs, that is, they unconditionally or reflexly elicit a variety of responses or patterns of behaviour; but they also act as incentives or goals, which animals will work to obtain (or avoid). These two sets of properties lie at the root of the two different ways that conditioning can produce changes in behaviour.

According to Pavlov, the reason why a CS-reinforcer association produces a conditional reflex is because the CS comes to substitute for the reinforcer, thereby acquiring the ability to elicit the same pattern of behaviour – salivation, leg flexion, approach, withdrawal. If dry food in the mouth elicits salivation, a CS associated with that food will also elicit salivation; if the sight of food elicits approach and pecking in a hungry pigeon, a small visual stimulus associated with the delivery of food will equally elicit approach and pecking.

According to Thorndike the principle of instrumental conditioning is the law of effect. A response that produces one class of consequence (roughly, appetitive reinforcers or rewards) will increase in probability; one that produces another class (roughly, aversive reinforcers or punishers) will decrease in probability. Instrumental responses are modified by their consequences, as opposed to Pavlovian CRs, which are simply elicited by a stimulus regardless of their consequences.

There is good reason to accept both Pavlov's and Thorndike's principles of reinforcement. Pavlov is right, because some responses are acquired regardless of their consequences. A dog that salivates to a CS signalling the delivery of food will still salivate even if the experimenter arranges that food never occurs on those trials when the dog salivates in advance of the normal time for its delivery (Herendeen & Shapiro, 1975). The law of effect predicts that dogs should learn *not* to salivate under these circumstances when exposed to this omission contingency, but this is something they seem to find remarkably difficult to do. Similar results have been obtained with other animals and other CRs (Mackintosh, 1983, pp. 30–33). But the Pavlovian principle is quite insufficient to account for all changes in behaviour in all conditioning experiments. For a start, it predicts that only responses elicited by (or at least related to) the reinforcer will be successfully conditioned: it should be impossible for animals to learn to perform wholly arbitrary responses to obtain food or avoid pain. Now it is true that animals often find it difficult to learn an operant response incompatible with their natural reactions to the reinforcer: Breland and Breland (1966) and Boakes, Poli, Lockwood, and Goodall (1978) reported that raccoons and rats were reluctant to drop a ball down a chute in order to obtain food. The problem was that the ball, by virtue of its association with food, elicited food-related CRs: the raccoons rubbed it between their paws, the rats put it in their mouth. While this is testimony to the power of the Pavlovian principle of reinforcement, it does not show it is an all-encompassing account of conditioning: Boakes et al.

10

(1978), for example, reported that all their rats *did* eventually learn to perform the required operant response.

A rat's lever presses for food or water rewards, or to escape or avoid shock, are not particularly closely related to any of these reinforcers, and since operant contingencies can determine the force, duration, and direction of such responses (Mackintosh, 1983, pp. 41, 138; see also Heyes & Dawson, 1990), it is hard to see how one could deny the operant principle of the law of effect. Moreover, although rats may come to approach and make contact with a manipulandum whose appearance signals the delivery of food, they will rapidly learn to avoid such responses if they cause the omission of food (Locurto, Terrace, & Gibbon, 1976): contrast this outcome with those referred to earlier, where Pavlovian CRs may persist for a long time even though they cause the omission of an appetitive reinforcer.

The distinction between classical and operant conditioning cannot then be merely operational. Some responses appear to be modifiable by their consequences while others seem to be simply elicited by a stimulus associated with a reinforcer regardless of those consequences. The distinction between these two processes is not an absolute one: although many responses may be affected more by one process than by the other, many are affected by both. In the final analysis, the question at issue is not whether a particular response is modifiable only by a stimulus–reinforcer contingency and another response only by a response–reinforcer contingency, it is whether we can separate the effects of the two types of contingencies.

Dickinson (1989) and his colleagues have revealed a further striking difference between Pavlovian and operant conditioning in the way in which a change in the incentive value of the reinforcer is translated into a change in behaviour. If a hungry dog receives conditioning trials with a CS paired with the delivery of meat powder, the salivary CR that emerges will show immediate and appropriate sensitivity to variations in the animal's level of motivation. If satiated for food, the dog will neither swallow the meat powder nor salivate to the CS signalling its delivery. But for an instrumental response to change in this way, the animal must, at some time or other, have had direct experience of the reinforcer under the changed level of motivation. Hungry rats trained to press a lever for sucrose (a reinforcer they have never experienced before) will continue to press the lever when satiated, unless and until they have the opportunity to discover that sucrose is of no value when they are satiated (Balleine, 1992). Similarly, the experiment described earlier on revaluing sucrose pellets by pairing their consumption with an injection of lithium has an immediate effect on Pavlovian CRs, but will produce a decline in instrumental responding only if the rat has a second opportunity to taste the sucrose after its initial pairing with illness (Balleine & Dickinson, 1991). Although these results are both surprising and perhaps puzzling, they certainly strengthen the case for arguing that there is an important distinction between the relatively automatic way in which an association between a CS and reinforcer allows the CS to elicit a change in behaviour, and the more indirect way in which an association between a response and a reinforcer causes a change in the probability of that response.

HIERARCHICAL ASSOCIATIONS

In a typical operant conditioning experiment, rats' lever presses are reinforced at some times but not at others, with the occurrence of reinforcement being marked by a particular discriminative stimulus (see Figure 3a). In due course the rat will learn to respond only in the presence of that stimulus. How is this control exercised? Some theorists have argued that there is a hierarchical or second-order association between the discriminative stimulus and the response–reinforcer relationship: in associative terms, the discriminative stimulus retrieves a representation of the response–reinforcer association (Mackintosh, 1983; Rescorla, 1991). Rescorla has provided evidence for this view with an experiment on blocking. Recall that blocking occurs when an added stimulus signals no change in reinforcement from that already predicted by the first stimulus. In general terms, the blocking experiment provides a powerful technique for inferring how animals encode information about the occurrence of a reinforcer. If blocking is disrupted by a particular change in the conditions under which reinforcement occurs, we can be confident that animals have detected this change. In the first stage of his experiments (as shown in Table 3) Rescorla trained rats in the presence of a single discriminative stimulus (S1) to perform two different responses, R1 and R2, for two different reinforcers Rf1 and Rf2. He then added a second stimulus, either maintaining the same relationship between responses and reinforcers as had been signalled by S1, or reversing that relationship so that now R1 was reinforced by Rf2 and R2 by Rf1. Where the compound signalled exactly the same relationship between response and reinforcer as S1 alone had, the added

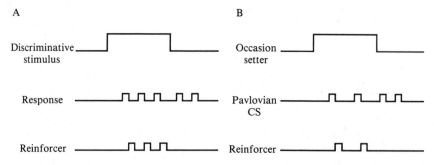

Figure 3 Diagrammatic representation of the relationship between a discriminative stimulus, response and reinforcer (A) and between an occasion setter, Pavlovian CS and reinforcer (B)

12

Table 3 Design and results of Rescorla (1991)

Group	Stage 1	Stage 2	Test results
Blocked	[S1: R1 → Rf1	[S1 + S2: R1 → Rf1	S2 does not control
	[S1: R2 → Rf2	[S1 + S2: R2 → Rf2	responding
Control	[S1: R1 → Rf2	[S1 + S2: R1 → Rf1	S2 does control
	[S1: R2 → Rf1	[S1 + S2: R2 → Rf2	responding

stimulus acquired no control over responding. But where the response–reinforcer relationships were changed, the added stimulus did acquire such control. Note that the only change was in the *relationship* between responses and reinforcers; any direct association between this stimulus and the response or the stimulus and the reinforcer alone was held constant across the two conditions. This study thus provides strong evidence that discriminative stimuli encode the actual relationship between events occurring in their presence.

Analogous effects have been discovered in Pavlovian experiments. A CS paired with a given reinforcer will be associated with that reinforcer, but if (as is shown in Figure 3b) this CS-reinforcer relationship holds only when another stimulus is present, then the second stimulus (the "occasion setter") may acquire hierarchical control over the first-order CS-reinforcer association; the first-order CS will elicit its CR only in the presence of the occasion setter (Holland, 1985; Rescorla, 1985). Of course, other simpler explanations of the establishment of this discrimination are possible, for it might be enough to say that both stimuli are associated with the reinforcer but too weakly for either to elicit a CR on its own. When both are combined, their combined associative strength is greater than some critical threshold and a CR occurs. But it turns out that the occasion setter's ability to control a CR to a target CS can survive substantial changes in its own direct association with the reinforcer. Under some conditions at least, repeated presentation of the occasion setter alone, sufficient to extinguish any such direct associations it may have, does not abolish its ability to control responding to its target CS (Holland, 1991).

There is evidence that the experimental context in which conditioning trials occur can also exert this sort of hierarchical control over associations between a CS or a response and reinforcer (Bouton & Swartzentruber, 1986). Under some circumstances (although by no means all), the effects of a series of conditioning or extinction trials may be largely confined to the context in which they occurred (Hall & Honey, 1990) and if different contingencies between CSs and reinforcers are established in different contexts, animals appear to retrieve the appropriate contingency when placed in the appropriate context.

13

ASSOCIATIVE LEARNING IN HUMANS

The time is long past when a learning theory based on conditioning experiments with animals was regarded as the key to understanding human behaviour. Many cognitive psychologists have taken it for granted that they could safely ignore both the results of, and the theories derived from, such experiments. Of course, it was acknowledged, CRs such as the eyeblink or GSR can be conditioned and extinguished, and may even show other phenomena found in animal studies (Lovibond, 1988; Martin & Levey, 1991); but what did this have to say of any interest to those studying human learning and memory, let alone thinking, reasoning, or problem solving? In normal adults, the conditioning process can apparently be overridden by instructions: simply telling subjects that the US will not occur again causes instant loss of a CR which would otherwise extinguish only slowly (Davey, 1983). Most subjects in a conditioning experiment are aware of the experimenter's contingencies, and in the absence of such awareness often fail to show evidence of conditioning (Brewer, 1974; but see Baeyens, Eelen, Van den Bergh, & Crombez, 1990, for an important exception to this generalization). Moreover, there are important differences between very young or severely retarded children (on the one hand) and older children and adults (on the other) in their behaviour in a variety of operant conditioning and discrimination learning experiments, differences that seem largely attributable to the development of language (Bentall & Lowe, 1987; Dugdale & Lowe, 1990). All this suggests that people have rather more efficient, language- or rule-based forms of learning at their disposal than the laborious formation of associations between a CS and a US. Even behaviour therapy, one of the apparently more successful attempts to apply principles of conditioning to human affairs, has given way to cognitive behaviour therapy or simply cognitive therapy.

The rise of connectionist theories has perhaps done something to change this perception, for such theories have provided surprisingly powerful explanations of many apparently complex aspects of human cognition (McClelland & Rumelhart, 1986; Morris, 1989; Rumelhart & McClelland, 1986) and have done so by applying little more than some of the basic assumptions of associative learning theory – including an error-correcting learning rule formally identical to that embodied in the Rescorla–Wagner model. The important message here is that it is probably less interesting to look for evidence of simple conditioning in human subjects than to apply the fundamental principles of associative learning (derived from conditioning experiments) to more complex situations. Thus Shanks and Dickinson (1987) have been able to show that the way in which people make judgements about contingencies between events (was one event the cause of another?) can be largely explained by the applications of the Rescorla–Wagner model (see also Wasserman, 1990), while Gluck and Bower (1988) and Shanks (1990) have

applied a similar analysis to the way in which people make diagnostic judgements or learn to sort stimuli into different categories, and McLaren, Kaye, and Mackintosh (1989) and Hall (1991) have argued that some simple principles of associative learning can successfully explain many of the well-known, but poorly understood, phenomena of perceptual learning both in people and in other animals. It is not too fanciful to detect opportunities for significant rapprochement between a variety of different areas within experimental psychology.

FURTHER READING

Dickinson, A. (1980). *Contemporary animal learning theory*. Cambridge: Cambridge University Press.

Domjan, M., & Burkhardt, B. (1986). *The principles of learning and behavior* (2nd edn). Pacific Grove, CA: Brooks/Cole.

Flaherty, C. F. (1985). *Animal learning and cognition*. New York: McGraw-Hill.

Mackintosh, N. J. (1974). *The psychology of animal learning*. London: Academic Press.

Mackintosh, N. J. (1983). *Conditioning and associative learning*. Oxford: Oxford University Press.

Pearce, J. M. (1987). *Introduction to animal cognition*. Hillsdale, NJ: Lawrence Erlbaum.

REFERENCES

Baeyens, F., Eelen, P., van den Bergh, O., & Crombez, G. (1990). Flavor–flavor and color–flavor conditioning in humans. *Learning and Motivation, 21*, 434–455.

Balleine, B. W. (1992). Instrumental performance following a shift in primary motivation depends on incentive learning. *Journal of Experimental Psychology: Animal Behavior Processes, 18*, 236–250.

Balleine, B. W., & Dickinson, A. (1991). Instrumental performance following reinforcer devaluation depends upon incentive learning. *Quarterly Journal of Experimental Psychology, 43B*, 279–296.

Bentall, R. P., & Lowe, C. F. (1987). The role of verbal behavior in human learning: III. Instructional effects in children. *Journal of the Experimental Analysis of Behavior, 47*, 177–190.

Boakes, R. A., Poli, M., Lockwood, M. J., & Goodall, G. (1978). A study of misbehavior: Token reinforcement in the rat. *Journal of the Experimental Analysis of Behavior, 29*, 115–134.

Bouton, M. E., & Swartzentruber, D. (1986). Analysis of the associative and occasion-setting properties of contexts participating in a Pavlovian discrimination. *Journal of Experimental Psychology: Animal Behavior Processes, 12*, 333–350.

Breland, K., & Breland, M. (1966). *Animal behavior*. New York: Macmillan.

Brewer, W. F. (1974). There is no convincing evidence for operant or classical conditioning in adult humans. In W. B. Weimer & D. S. Palermo (Eds) *Cognition and the symbolic processes* (pp. 1–42). Hillsdale, NJ: Lawrence Erlbaum.

Davy, G. C. L. (1983). An associative view of human classical conditioning. In G. C. L. Davey (Ed.) *Animal models of human behavior: Conceptual, evolutionary, and neurobiological perspectives* (pp. 95–114). Chichester: Wiley.

Dickinson, A. (1989). Expectancy theory in animal conditioning. In S. B. Klein & R. R. Mowrer (Eds) *Contemporary learning theories* (pp. 279–308). Hillsdale, NJ: Lawrence Erlbaum.

Dickinson, A., & Mackintosh, N. J. (1979). Reinforcer specificity in the enhancement of conditioning by post-trial surprise. *Journal of Experimental Psychology: Animal Behavior Processes, 5,* 162–177.

Dickinson, A., Watt, A., & Griffiths, W. J. H. (1992). Free-operant acquisition with delayed reinforcement. *Quarterly Journal of Experimental Psychology, 45B,* 241–258.

Dugdale, N., & Lowe, C. F. (1990). Naming and stimulus equivalence. In D. E. Blackman & H. Lejeune (Eds) *Behaviour analysis in theory and practice: Contributions and controversies* (pp. 115–138). Hillsdale, NJ: Lawrence Erlbaum.

Ferster, C. B., & Skinner, B. F. (1957). *Schedules of reinforcement.* New York: Appleton-Century-Crofts.

Garrud, P., Goodall, G., & Mackintosh, N. J. (1981). Overshadowing of a stimulus–reinforcer association by an instrumental response. *Quarterly Journal of Experimental Psychology, 33B,* 123–135.

Gibbon, J., Baldock, M. D., Locurto, C., Gold, L., & Terrace, H. S. (1977). Trial and intertrial durations in autoshaping. *Journal of Experimental Psychology: Animal Behavior Processes, 3,* 264–284.

Gluck, M. A., & Bower, G. H. (1988). From conditioning to category learning: An adaptive network model. *Journal of Experimental Psychology: General, 117,* 227–247.

Hall, G. (1991). *Perceptual and associative learning.* Oxford: Oxford University Press.

Hall, G., & Honey, R. C. (1990) Context-specific conditioning in the conditioned-emotional-response procedure. *Journal of Experimental Psychology: Animal Behavior Processes, 16,* 271–278.

Herendeen, D. L., & Shapiro, M. M. (1975). Extinction and food-reinforced inhibition of conditioned salivation in dogs. *Animal Learning and Behavior, 3,* 103–106.

Heyes, C. M., & Dawson, G. R. (1990). A demonstration of observational learning in rats using a bidirectional control. *Quarterly Journal of Experimental Psychology, 42B,* 59–72.

Holland, P. C. (1985). The nature of conditioned inhibition in serial and simultaneous feature negative discriminations. In R. R. Miller & N. E. Spear (Eds) *Information processing in animals: Conditioned inhibition* (pp. 267–297). Hillsdale, NJ: Lawrence Erlbaum.

Holland, P. C. (1991). Transfer of control in ambiguous discriminations. *Journal of Experimental Psychology: Animal Behavior Processes, 17,* 231–248.

Holland, P. C., & Straub, J. J. (1979). Differential effects of two ways of devaluing the unconditioned stimulus after Pavlovian appetitive conditioning. *Journal of Experimental Psychology: Animal Behavior Processes, 5,* 65–78.

Kamin, L. J. (1969). Predictability, surprise, attention and conditioning. In R. Campbell & R. Church (Eds) *Punishment and aversive behaviour* (pp. 279–296). New York: Appleton-Century-Crofts.

Locurto, C., Terrace, H. S., & Gibbon, J. (1976). Autoshaping, random control, and omission training in the rat. *Journal of the Experimental Analysis of Behavior, 26,* 451–462.

Lovibond, P. F. (1988). Predictive validity in human causal judgment and Pavlovian conditioning. *Biosocial Psychology, 27,* 79–93.

McClelland, J. L., & Rumelhart, D. E. (1986). *Parallel distributed processing: Explorations in the microstructure of cognition*, vol. II. Cambridge, MA: Bradford.

Mackintosh, N. J. (1983). *Conditioning and associative learning*. Oxford: Oxford University Press.

Mackintosh, N. J., & Dickinson, A. (1979). Instrumental (Type II) conditioning. In A. Dickinson & R. A. Boakes (Eds) *Mechanisms of learning and motivation* (pp. 143–167). Hillsdale, NJ: Lawrence Erlbaum.

McLaren, I. P. L., Kaye, H., & Mackintosh, N. J. (1989). An associative theory of the representation of stimuli: applications to perceptual learning and latent inhibition. In R. G. M. Morris (Ed.) *Parallel distributed processing: Implications for psychology and neurobiology* (pp. 102–130). Oxford: Oxford University Press.

Martin, I., & Levey, A. B. (1991). Blocking observed in human eyelid conditioning. *Quarterly Journal of Experimental Psychology, 43B*, 233–256.

Miller, S., & Konorski, J. (1928). "Sur une forme particulière des réflexes conditionnels". *Comptes rendus des séances de la société de biologie, 99*, 1155–1157.

Morris, R. G. M. (Ed.) (1989). *Parallel distributed processing: Implications for psychology and neurobiology*. Oxford: Oxford University Press.

Pavlov, I. P. (1927). *Conditioned reflexes*. Oxford: Oxford University Press.

Rescorla, R. A. (1968). Probability of shock in the presence and absence of CS in fear conditioning. *Journal of Comparative and Physiological Psychology, 66*, 1–5.

Rescorla, R. A. (1969). Pavlovian conditioned inhibition. *Psychological Bulletin, 72*, 77–94.

Rescorla, R. A. (1985). Conditioned inhibition and facilitation. In R. R. Miller & N. E. Spear (Eds) *Information processing in animals: Conditioned inhibition* (pp. 299–326). Hillsdale, NJ: Lawrence Erlbaum.

Rescorla, R. A. (1991). Associative relations in instrumental learning. *Quarterly Journal of Experimental Psychology, 43B*, 1–24.

Rescorla, R. A., & Wagner, A. R. (1972). A theory of Pavlovian conditioning: Variations in the effectiveness of reinforcement and nonreinforcement. In A. H. Black & W. F. Prokasy (Eds) *Classical conditioning II: Current research and theory* (pp. 64–99). New York: Appleton-Century-Crofts.

Revusky, S. (1971). The role of interference in association over a delay. In W. K. Honig & P. H. R. James (Eds) *Animal memory* (pp. 155–213). New York: Academic Press.

Revusky, S., & Garcia, J. (1970). Learned associations over long delays. In G. H. Bower (Ed.) *The psychology of learning and motivation* (vol. 4, pp. 1–84). New York: Academic Press.

Rozin, P., & Kalat, J. W. (1971). Specific hungers and poisoning as adaptive specializations of learning. *Psychological Review, 78*, 459–486.

Rumelhart, D. E., & McClelland, J. L. (1986). *Parallel distributed processing: Explorations in the microstructure of cognition*, vol. I. Cambridge, MA; Bradford.

Seligman, M. E. P. (1970). On the generality of the laws of learning. *Psychological Review, 77*, 406–418.

Shanks, D. R. (1990). Connectionism and the learning of probabilistic concepts. *Quarterly Journal of Experimental Psychology, 42A*, 209–238.

Shanks, D. R., & Dickinson, A. (1987). Associative accounts of causality judgment. In G. H. Bower (Ed.) *The psychology of learning and motivation* (vol. 21, pp. 229–261). San Diego, CA: Academic Press.

Skinner, B. F. (1938). *The behavior of organisms*. New York: Appleton-Century-Crofts.

Thorndike, E. L. (1911). *Animal intelligence: Experimental studies*. New York: Macmillan.

Wasserman, E. A. (1990). Detecting response–outcome relations: Toward an understanding of the causal texture of the environment. In G. H. Bower (Ed.) *The psychology of learning and motivation: Advances in research and theory* (vol. 26, pp. 27–82). London: Academic Press.

APPLIED BEHAVIOUR ANALYSIS

Donald M. Baer
University of Kansas, USA

Reinforcement concepts and techniques in applied behaviour analysis	Technological
	Conceptually systematic
	Effective
The definition of applied behaviour analysis	Capable of generalized effects
	Summary
Applied	**Further reading**
Behavioural	**References**
Analytic	

Many practitioners would agree that they practise applied behaviour analysis, but some of them would not agree completely on the definition of their discipline, or that other practitioners who claim to be applied behaviour analysts deserve the title. Of course, that kind of disagreement is true of many disciplines, applied and basic. In the case of applied behaviour analysis, diversity of opinion probably results from a pre-existing diversity in the philosophical approach, behaviourism, from which it is derived, and in the diverse trainings and motivations of its practitioners and researchers.

Zuriff (1985), in *Behaviorism*, reviews the wide variety of logic and definition that operate in modern behaviourism. He shows that even so, a consistent enough core of usage, argument, and procedure can be extracted to define at least one philosophical approach deserving the name; his book is aptly subtitled *A Conceptual Reconstruction*. Much the same deconstructive-reconstructive approach is needed to characterize applied behaviour analysis, because it shows a large overlap with, yet certain small differences from, related disciplines called behaviour modification, behaviour therapy, cognitive-behaviour therapy, cognitive therapy, learning theory, social learning theory, radical behaviourism, methodological behaviourism, neo-behaviourism, and the like.

Inspecting the tables of contents of two definitive texts, *Contemporary Behavior Therapy*, edited by Wilson and Franks (1982), and *Theoretical Issues in Behavior Therapy*, edited by Reiss and Bootzin (1985), will illustrate this breadth. It will also suggest that disciplinary diversity is increasing rather than condensing to an essential core. Those texts will show the reader the larger context of behavioural application, which makes discussion of any one of its variants somewhat arbitrary. However, careful reading of those chapters may also show that although practitioners display great diversity in discussing the meaning of their work, the work itself shows considerably less diversity.

REINFORCEMENT CONCEPTS AND TECHNIQUES IN APPLIED BEHAVIOUR ANALYSIS

In its early years, applied behaviour analysis was mainly an attempt to see whether learning theory, until then essentially a laboratory science based mainly on studies of animal behaviour, could be applied to the problems of real people in their society. The basic principle in learning theory appeared to be reinforcement: whether a behaviour will occur more or less frequently in the future is determined most fundamentally by certain of its consistent, systematic consequences (cf. Skinner, 1938, 1953). Those consequences that affect the future occurrence of the behaviours that precede them are termed *reinforcers*, simply to label the fact that they affect the behaviours that precede them. Some of them are called *positive reinforcers* because they increase the future probability of responses that consistently and systematically produce or increase them, and others of them are called *negative reinforcers* because they increase the future probability of responses that consistently and systematically avoid or reduce them. Increasing a behaviour's future probability by controlling its consequences in either process is termed *reinforcement*. When reinforcement is discontinued, that increased probability of the behaviour's occurrence typically declines to its pre-reinforcement level, and that process is usually termed *extinction*.

Thus, for example, we may discover that many of a person's behaviours exist because they often achieve approval from important other people, and we may then call approval a positive reinforcer for those behaviours of that person; we may discover that many others of the person's behaviours exist because they often avoid or reduce disapproval from important other people, and we may then call disapproval a negative reinforcer for those behaviours of that person; and we may well see that many of those behaviours, once strong, are lost or reduced when they no longer accomplish either process.

If reinforcement is the basic principle of learning theory, then *discrimination* is its most important derivative principle (cf. Skinner, 1938, 1953). The

20

point of discrimination is that in real life, no behaviour leads to the same consistent, systematic consequences at all times and in all places. For example, even breathing does not always produce its natural consequence of the oxygen-nitrogen-pollutants mixture that we call air. Swimming requires that breathing occurs only when the mouth or nostrils are out of the water; singing requires, somewhat less stringently, that we breathe according to the structure of the music rather than at any time we may be a little short of breath. In swimming, the relevant reinforcer is access to the air; in singing, the relevant positive reinforcer is the maximal beauty of the music we produce, and the relevant negative reinforcers are our disapproval (and our audience's disapproval) of any breathing patterns that would mar that beauty.

If there are environmental events – stimuli – that mark the times or places when a behaviour will have consistent, systematic reinforcing consequences, then those stimuli typically will come to evoke those behaviours that will produce or increase positive reinforcers at those times or places, or evoke those behaviours that will avoid or reduce negative reinforcers at those times or places. Thus "out of water" and "end of phrase" are stimuli signalling when breathing will have reinforcing consequences; they are termed *discriminative stimuli* to index the fact that they control our behaviour in that way.

A more fundamental statement is possible: what we mean by learning is behaviour change. What we mean by behaviour change is the selection of some behaviours over others. Learning theory argues that environments select behaviours, and put them under the control of any stimuli that may mark when or where the selection processes operate. The behaviours that environments select are those that produce and increase, or avoid and reduce, the relevant consequences of that environment – its reinforcers. That argument resembles evolutionary theory, which supposes that environments select most the species that survive well enough in them to reproduce best. Over generations, evolution selects species sensitive to certain reinforcers relevant to survival and reproduction, and capable of becoming sensitive to even more; within any organism's life, reinforcers select the behaviours that best produce or avoid them. Both approaches are thereby seen as *selectionist* in philosophy.

Despite the pervasiveness of the reinforcement concept and its techniques in applied behaviour analysis, they are not definitional of it. However, they may well seem so to casual inspection of the field; a very large proportion of conceptualization and practice in the field embodies them. So, while they are not definitional, their frequent operation in the discipline sometimes makes behaviour-analytic diagnosis and intervention rather distinctive, considered alongside more traditional psychological approaches, and that distinctiveness needs description here.

In traditional approaches, problem behaviour is very likely to be seen as expressive; if so, its form or topography becomes a key to its meaning. By contrast, in applied behaviour analysis (as in its parent disciplines, behaviour analysis and operant psychology), behaviour is invariably questioned first for its instrumentality – for what consequences it accomplishes in the behaver's environment. In that case, its form becomes almost irrelevant, because different environments can easily give the same function to an arbitrary range of behaviour topographies.

The aggressive child is a classic example. Suppose that a child in a day-care setting often hits, scratches, pushes, and bites other children, often destroys their constructions and possessions, and often threatens them with these and other forms of violence. Traditional views usually begin with the topography of the child's behaviour, see it as aggressive and destructive, and suppose that it is expressive. The usual assumption is that aggression expresses anger, resentment, or fear. Then a traditional diagnosis asks what has made this child angry, resentful, or afraid (and perhaps singles out what seems a relevant fact, such as a new baby in the family). Subsequent therapy often focuses on reducing those causes (e.g., telling parents to increase their attention to this child, despite the new baby), and perhaps considers teaching the child to respond to them better (e.g., tells the parents to make the child an extravagantly praised helper in caring for the baby). A behaviour-analytic approach asks instead what consequences these behaviours consistently, systematically accomplish, and relies on extensive, intensive, objective, uninterpretative observation to see what they may be.

That kind of observation, to be behavioural, requires the observer to count how often and how long, and where and when, certain physically defined behaviours occur, whether or not they seem to meet the spirit in which the observation is undertaken. Again, the aggressive child is a classic example. An observer of aggression would not be asked to record the child's "aggressions" (and its consequences); that would require interpretation, and we would find ourselves studying the observer's interpretative behaviour, not the child's aggressions. Instead, the observer very likely would be asked to observe all instances of "forceful application of hands/feet/teeth/shoulders to the body/property of another person". That kind of definition is meant to prevent interpretation by the observer. It also allows a small amount of invalid measurement, as, for example, if the child plays a friendly game of leap-frog and necessarily applies hands forcefully to the back of another child. In the applied behaviour-analytic approach, the occasional error of that kind is considered a small price for a better approximation to objectivity of measurement.

A beginning list of the systematic consequences of aggression, so defined, that objective observation often will reveal might take the following form:

1 intense, lengthy, sympathetic adult attention
2 intense, lengthy, angry adult attention

3 a temporary lapse in the ongoing demands for work or obedience that adults make on well-behaved children
4 undisputed control of some play space
5 undisputed control of some play materials
6 solitude
7 tears, crying, and retreats by other children.

Any of these systematic consequences may be the positive or negative reinforcer supporting this behaviour, or the reinforcer may be something else that the observer has not yet noticed. And there may be more than one reinforcer operative in this case.

When the list is considered complete, the observer will often ask a helpful question about each item on it: "Do any other easily performed behaviours of the child seem to accomplish this consequence better (more reliably, more quickly, more enduringly, with less effort) than the aggressive behaviours under study?" The answer may already be evident, or it may require further observation. If the answer is Yes, the probability diminishes that this item is the reinforcer responsible for the frequent aggressive behaviour, but not to zero; if the answer is No, the probability rises that this item is the responsible reinforcer, but not to certainty. The question is helpful, but not definitive.

In applied behaviour analysis, the only certain way to decide among these reinforcer possibilities is to perform a set of diagnostic experiments, often called a functional *analysis* (e.g., Carr & Durand, 1985; Iwata, Pace, Kalsher, Caldery, & Cataldo, 1990). These experiments require first that each consequence be controlled systematically, one at a time, to reveal what will happen to the aggressive behaviours when they no longer accomplish this particular consequence. The preceding question can help establish the most cost-effective order in which to test these possibilities. In addition, these experiments require that careful, extensive observation establish if the aggressive behaviour occurs similarly throughout all the child's environments, or only in some places; and whether it occurs similarly at all times, or only at some times.

The combination of answers from these two classes of experiments should guide the intervention that will follow. For example, suppose that the experiments show that it is the consistently consequent lengthy attention from teachers at day-care and parents at home, whether approving or disapproving, that is the reinforcer. Suppose the observations show that aggressive behaviours from this child are seen primarily when teachers or parents are available to answer them with lengthy attention. That pattern means that one appropriate intervention is to discontinue those parental and teacher patterns, so that aggression no longer consistently and systematically produces attention from teachers and parents. Yet aggression cannot simply be ignored, for fear that children will be hurt; thus the parents and teachers may be taught to attend immediately, consistently, and systematically to the aggressor's victim rather than to the aggressor, removing the victim from harm as instantly as possible without a moment's attention to the aggressor (e.g., Pinkston, Reese, LeBlanc, & Baer, 1973). In addition, teachers and parents may be taught to consistently and systematically offer lengthy attention for desirable non-aggressive behaviours by this child, so that the same reinforcer can be gained by child behaviours that are not only more desirable to all, but also easier for the child.

Alternatively, suppose that the experiments show that it is the undisputed control of certain toys and materials that is the reinforcer, and the observations show that aggression is seen only when those particular toys and materials are available for play. Then the intervention could take the form of never making those toys and materials available, or of making sure that aggression always forfeits their control to children other than the aggressor, meanwhile making certain that the child knows better ways to ask to use those toys and materials, and that those ways will prove more efficient than aggression in future access to them.

Alternatively again, suppose that the experiments show that the reinforcer is the sight and sound of other children crying and retreating, and the observations show that aggression against them occurs at any times they are present. Then the intervention may take the form of reducing the reinforcing effectiveness of those particular reinforcers, and increasing the reinforcing effectiveness of their opposites. Two assumptions will be made. One is that these reinforcers have acquired their reinforcing function through unfortunate socialization experiences. The other is that the discrimination process can be used to make and unmake reinforcers: its formulas are that stimuli made discriminative for access to positive reinforcers or escape from negative reinforcers usually become positive reinforcers themselves, that stimuli made discriminative for the loss of positive reinforcers or gaining of negative reinforcers usually become negative reinforcers themselves, and that when stimuli lose their discriminative function, they usually also lose the reinforcing function that discriminative function had lent them (cf. Catania, 1984, pp. 179–185; Kazdin, 1977, p. 3; Reese, 1978, p. 21; Skinner, 1953, chap. 12; Stubbs & Cohen, 1972). Then the intervention might well be to create an environment in which when other children are happy, this child has maximal access to as many as possible of his or her other reinforcers; and when other children cry or run away, this child has as minimal access as possible to as many as possible of his or her other reinforcers.

However, applied behaviour analysis is often practised when prior functional analysis of a problem behaviour is impossible, impractical, or not favoured by the practitioner. (It can be problematic to conduct the necessary experiments and observations in real-life settings, and when they are done in more convenient settings instead, it is easy to doubt their validity for the real-life settings in which the behaviour under investigation is a problem.) In those cases, interventions probably will not attempt to change the current reinforcement contingencies, but instead will try to override their effects with more powerful reinforcement contingencies developed and applied by the practitioner. Many behaviours have been altered effectively by the contingent use of approval and praise, sweets and other favoured edibles, access to specially favoured activities, money, and the like, all without analysis of what reinforcers (if any) were maintaining the problem behaviour.

Indeed, the frequent success of money as a positive reinforcer, when used in adequate amounts, parallels a classic technique in applied behaviour analysis to achieve similar success by mimicking its essential characteristics: the *token reinforcement system* or *token economy* (cf. Kazdin, 1977; Martin & Pear, 1978, pp. 137, 144–145, 335–365). A token economy is constructed by maintaining a shop or store that stocks every practical reinforcer known to be even occasionally effective for the people under study, whether these are tangible things or tickets allowing access to special activities; these are called the *back-ups*, and if possible they are made unavailable from any other source. Back-ups can be bought only with a special currency, the token. Tokens are often small pieces of plastic that token-system clients can get only through the practitioner; sometimes, they are simply marks entered in the client's account book by the practitioner; and sometimes they are merely verbal announcements of having earned points toward something.

The practitioner assigns in advance how many tokens are required to purchase each item in the store, and makes that known to the clients, either by posting prices if the clients have the necessary cognitive skills, or through extensive experience if they do not. If the store is well stocked for the clients at hand, and if the practitioner has successfully taught the clients that these items are available only by purchasing them with tokens, that is, through token exchanges, and has taught the clients all of what back-ups are available, and at what cost, then the token itself becomes an exceptionally powerful reinforcer.

Any client's reinforcers vary in effectiveness from time to time, and from situation to situation; and of course any client may become temporarily satiated with one reinforcer or another. The effectiveness of the token system results from the great variety of potential reinforcers that it stocks, such that there is sure to be at least one effective reinforcer for any client at any time, and very likely to be many. The practicality of the token system is equally great: practitioners can readily carry and dispense tokens as contingent reinforcers, when they could hardly carry or dispense many of the back-ups that the tokens will buy (such as access to a public game, or a container of cold soda, or an hour's TV viewing time, or a hamburger). With tokens, practitioners have the opportunity not only to reinforce the responses they have chosen as clinically desirable for the client, immediately as they occur, but also to teach needful clients the skills of collecting, keeping safe, and eventually exchanging tokens, thereby slowly moving the clients from dependence on only short-term gratifications to much longer-term ones.

Even so, the practitioner can easily diminish the value of the tokens by requiring too many of them for the back-ups, by requiring too few of them for the back-ups, by constantly changing prices, by reducing the critical variety of the back-ups, by not maintaining a balance of high-priced and low-priced items, by delaying tokens-for-back-ups exchange times too long for the clients' current abilities to mediate, by not teaching clients the skills necessary to avoid misplacing their accumulating tokens, by allowing some clients to be systematically victimized by others who steal their tokens, or by not keeping up with the clients' changing tastes as the behaviour-change programme proceeds.

Token systems have often been criticized as being artificial, and as teaching inappropriately materialistic values (often by critics whose own behaviour is thoroughly and happily enmeshed in the money system of their culture). In response to these criticisms, many applied behaviour analysts have given up their use, despite their power for otherwise difficult-to-accomplish behaviour changes. Others have learned to use token systems only temporarily, and have them gradually fade out of noticeable existence, at first by systematically making the exchanges later and later. Meanwhile, they begin to replace the physical token awards with symbolic account-book awards and a great deal of approval. Then their approval grows steadily more prominent as the account-book awards grow less prominent and less reliable. Soon, merely very approving verbal agreements about roughly how many tokens have been earned are operating, thus making the eventual exchanges less on the basis of how much credit the client has amassed, and more on the basis of how well the client has behaved since the last exchange. Indeed those two criteria have become essentially identical, and the system has become remarkably like those ordinary, undesigned everyday social systems in which people who behave well are treated well. When applied to developmentally delayed clients, this cosmetic fading of the token system into an unobtrusive natural social arrangement will go more slowly, in part because it will require the early teaching of the necessary cognitive skills before the explicit token system can fade into the implicit one, if it is to remain successful.

Using principles and procedures much like these, or derivative from these, applied behaviour analysts (sometimes using other professional titles) have since the early 1970s made and published several thousand experimental analyses of many problematic behaviours in a wide variety of clients at a wide variety of age levels. The following list notes illustrative examples of the behaviours that have often been targeted:

aggression	biting
alcoholism	blood pressure
anger	bullying
assertiveness	community organization
attendance	compliance
attention span	cooperation

counting
courtesy
door-slamming
drug abuse
elective mutism
energy conservation
enuresis
exercise
grammar
greeting others
hair-pulling
headbanging
heart-rate
hyperactivity
imitation
littering
marital discord
on-task behaviour
over-eating
peer-tutoring
pill-taking
play skills
posture
promptness

property destruction
public speaking
quarrelling
recruiting praise
safety
seizures
self-injury
self-instruction
self-monitoring
self-scratching
sentence construction
sign language
sloppiness
smoking
social skills
staff training
study
tantrums
teasing
thumbsucking
vandalism
volunteering
vomiting
walking skills

The next list notes the settings in which these behaviours have most often been changed:

clinics
delinquency halfway houses
factories
homes
hospitals
mental hospitals
nursing stations
offices
playgrounds
preschool classrooms

public school classrooms
public spaces
retardation halfway houses
retardation institutions
shops and malls
street intersections
streets
university classrooms
waiting rooms

Somewhat more detailed accounts of just how these behaviours were changed in the people living or working in these settings can be gleaned from several texts designed to provide overviews of the field, notably those by Sulzer-Azaroff and Mayer (1991), Martin and Pear (1978), and Reese (1978). Readers will note that the most frequently used techniques are based on the reinforcement and discrimination principles just sketched. Despite its heavy reliance on them, reinforcement concepts and techniques are not definitional of applied behaviour analysis. But, with an appreciation of their prevalence in the discipline, we are in a better position to consider how to define it.

THE DEFINITION OF APPLIED BEHAVIOUR ANALYSIS

The first research journal devoted to the discipline of applied behaviour analysis, the appropriately named *Journal of Applied Behavior Analysis*, was first published in 1968. In its first issue, Baer, Wolf, and Risley (1968) offered a tentative characterization of the field in its first article, "Some current dimensions of applied behavior analysis". That paper, which cited seven essential or ideal dimensions of then-current research and practice, has been widely cited since as either definitive or comprehensively characteristic of the discipline. Nearly twenty years later, an anniversary edition of the journal presented an updated version of that article (Baer, Wolf, & Risley, 1987), which cited the same seven dimensions, as prefaced by its title, "Some still-current dimensions of applied behavior analysis". It noted that twenty years of experience had not changed these seven dimensions, but had greatly broadened the contexts within which each was to be understood.

Those seven prescriptions are that work in the field should be *applied*, *behavioural*, *analytic*, *technological*, *conceptually systematic*, *effective*, and *capable of generalized effects*. Each of these is discussed below.

Applied

The analysis of behaviour is applied, if first, the behaviours under analysis can be categorized as a *problem* by at least the individual troubled by them and the practitioner to whom the troubled individual complains (on the assumption that the practitioner can change them); and second, changing those behaviours does indeed solve or alleviate the complainer's problem (cf. Baer, 1988). The application is perhaps more important if the behaviours are considered a problem by a larger segment of society, but a great deal of application is done for individuals.

It is important to note that especially in the areas of developmental disability and mental illness, and especially when the troubling behaviours reside in children, the people who complain most often to practitioners cite problems not with their own behaviours, but with the behaviours of the delayed or mentally ill individuals, or of the children, with whom they live or for whose habilitation, rehabilitation, or teaching they have been made responsible, or have assumed responsibility.

In this view, it is crucial to note that true application is not achieved simply by changing the targeted behaviours; it must also be true that changing those behaviours solves or alleviates the complainers' problem. In this approach, no behaviours are intrinsically pathological; their problematic status always depends on at least one complainer. A behaviour is problematic only because someone finds it so, or a culture defines it as such, and one or more practitioners agree to attempt its change. Even cultural definitions are contextual: there is hardly a behaviour to which we can object that would not be found

28

desirable or tolerable in some other context. We see killing as murder in a peaceful context but as heroism in a warlike context; we see a person's deliberate self-exposure to death as hurtful or sinful in some contexts, but heroic in others (as when trying to rescue a child from a burning building).

Behavioural

In behavioural application, behaviours are defined to be publicly observable by virtually any observer, rather than only by someone trained in the relevant clinical science. That means that only their physical dimensions will be cited as what the observer is to see or hear and record; it follows that behaviours that have no physical dimensions cannot be observed and so evade analysis and treatment in the discipline. As noted earlier, observers are never told to record something labelled "aggression", but instead something physical requiring much less interpretation on their part, for example "forceful application of hands/feet/teeth/shoulders to the body/property of another person". Similarly, observers usually are not asked to discriminate between "intentional" forceful applications and "accidental" forceful applications, unless we can specify some physical conditions that we believe will reliably separate the two categories. Some practitioners might risk defining "intentional" as only those that occur with an immediately prior (e.g., within 3 seconds) orientation of the aggressor's face to the subsequent target, and the rest as "unintentional"; other practitioners might see this as a reasonable attempt, but too fraught with potential error for ordinary use. This difference between practitioners' development of their measurement systems is one of pragmatic judgement, not principle.

However, if the postulate is that behaviours that have no physical dimensions, or no publicly observable physical dimensions, must be ignored by the discipline, that can lead to apparently principled disputes, and sometimes to invidious comparisons between behaviour-analytic and cognitive approaches. For example, when clients complain of persistent distressing thoughts that they do not know how to stop or prevent, it might appear that behavioural practitioners must on principle confess their helplessness while cognitive practitioners will recognize a problem exactly appropriate to their discipline. In practice, the difference will prove more verbal than real. Both will very likely teach essentially the same "thought-stopping" techniques (cf. Cautela & Wysocki, 1977). The cognitive analysts will report that their intervention was responsive to their clients' thoughts, and that they were successful in stopping those thoughts. The behavioural practitioners will report that their intervention was responsive to their clients' descriptions of their thoughts, and that they were successful in getting their clients to describe an absence of those thoughts. Very likely, both sets of practitioners will have done essentially the same things and have based their conclusions on essentially the same evidence. The cognitive analysts may be a little less troubled about the reality of what they had just accomplished, but not much. Theorists, of course, may continue to see a profound difference of paradigm in how the two sets of practitioners talk about their work.

Analytic

Behaviour analysis is analytic when first: it can convincingly show the origin of, or more likely, what is currently maintaining the problem behaviours under consideration; second, it can convincingly show that the procedures subsequently applied to the problem are responsible for the behaviour changes that occur; third, it makes good theoretical sense that those procedures should have changed those behaviours in that way; and fourth, those changes resolve or alleviate the original complaint about the behaviours to be changed. At their best, practice and research in the field achieve all four; but quite often, usually because of practical limitations, only the second and third are accomplished, and sometimes only the second.

To accomplish even the second − to show convincingly that the procedures applied to a set of behaviours are responsible for the subsequent changes in those behaviours − requires a small experiment. Typically, those experiments are conducted with one subject, the client; hence they use what are called single-subject designs. The single-subject designs, frequently used throughout the history of natural science, are rarely used in social, behavioural, and clinical sciences; thus their use gives applied behaviour analysis (and behaviour analysis) another quite distinctive attribute, and incidentally reveals its strong affinity for the natural rather than the social sciences. One quite common version of single-subject design uses four successive phases: first, the practitioner-researcher observes, measures, and plots the behaviours under study on to a graph, and establishes that measurement is reliable, that the behaviours do indeed have a level that can be considered a problem, and that there is no natural trend in these behaviours that would indicate that they will improve as fast as a practitioner might improve them. Second, an intervention is made: behaviour-change procedures are applied while measurement and graphing continue, to reveal whether these procedures are effective enough to satisfy the practitioner-researcher's judgement of how much change is needed, and how promptly it is needed. Third, if the procedures seem promising, then measurement and graphing continue while the behaviour-change procedures are discontinued, or are replaced by contrasting procedures (e.g., a "placebo"), to show whether the change just observed was coincidental or a systematic result of the behaviour-change procedures applied by the practitioner-researcher. Fourth, if the behaviour-change is reversed, diminished, or halted, then measurement and graphing continue while the behaviour-change procedures applied in the second phase are resumed, and the behaviours are brought to the final state of change desired by the practitioner-researcher, who is now confident that those behaviour changes are not coincidental, but are systematic results of the behaviour-change procedures applied.

An exposition of all of the single-subject designs, and all their procedures, would be prohibitively long here; interested readers might well begin their study with Kazdin's (1982) text, *Single-Case Research Designs*.

Technological

Applied behaviour analysis is presumed to be more of a scientific process than an artful or personal one. Thus, we would not expect it to be practised better by certain experts than others; its effective procedures should have been disseminated perfectly by way of research reports, manuals, training films, and tapes, etc. All its applications are supposed to become matters of recipe, much like the recipes of cookery books. Even modestly trained readers with relatively little experience should always be able to produce the same result simply by following the recipe.

Yet sometimes applied behaviour-analytic practitioner-researchers find that the presumably complete and objective descriptions of their procedures are not sufficient to allow reasonably trained readers to accomplish the same level of results. In that case, a highly appropriate next research target is to discover what ingredients are missing from the recipes that had been offered to the field previously, so as to publish new recipes that are more perfectly technological.

Devotion to technology gives much of the applied behaviour-analytic literature a distinctive character. Readers looking for exact solutions to behaviour-change problems may often find exactly what they need; readers in search of new principles will probably be bored.

Conceptually systematic

The conceptual system of a cookery book lies in physical chemistry, and very few cooks know enough physical chemistry to appreciate the unity and predictability of the recipes in any of their books. When enough properly technological recipes exist to satisfy virtually every eater's needs, cooks need not learn more. However, in a field like applied behaviour analysis, where not nearly enough recipes exist to solve the problems confronting practitioners, the field will advance better if its practitioners can become practitioner-researchers (cf. Pinkston, Levitt, Green, Linsk, & Rzepnicki, 1982, esp. chaps 2, 4, 9, and 10) who can refine existing recipes and invent the new ones necessary for some new problems. That is likely to proceed more efficiently if the practitioner-researchers have a conceptual system that explains how behaviour works, and does so well enough to predict what kinds of behaviour-change interventions are effective, what it may mean when they do not work as expected at first, and, most important of all, what to do next in that case. Many conceptual systems can explain anything that happens, once it is clear what has happened; far fewer seem able to explain a failure in terms that reliably indicate how to produce a subsequent success.

So far, the largely reinforcement-based conceptual system of applied behaviour analysis has met that criterion fairly well. However, it is obvious that if some alternative conceptual system could accomplish the same goals even better, applied behaviour analysts could immediately turn to that new system, and to its distinctive procedures, and still be applied behaviour analysts. Reinforcement theory is not the definitive characteristic of applied behaviour analysis; but one of the field's definitive characteristics is to rely on some conceptual system for these purposes.

Effective

Almost every clinical discipline aspires to effectiveness; the distinctive disciplinary question is how to define it. The internal logic of applied behaviour analysis suggests two sometimes distinctive meanings of effectiveness.

First, because in this approach no behaviour is intrinsically pathological, and problem behaviours are thought to be defined as such only by relevant people and cultural practice, then it follows that any behavioural intervention has been effective not to the extent that it has changed its target behaviours, but to the extent that it has changed the complaints about those target behaviours that provoked the behaviour-change intervention in the first place. Thus, in a school system that grades its students' work as A, B, C, D, and F (failing), changing the study and work behaviours of a student who is constantly awarded Fs into behaviours that will earn Ds will be effective enough, if the originating complaint is merely that the student is failing. If the originating complaint is that the student is shamefully stupid by ordinary social standards, then effectiveness may require that the behaviours be changed enough to achieve Cs. If the originating complaint is that the student will not be able to apply successfully to a medical school, then effectiveness will demand that the behaviours be changed into those that earn As.

Second, even if a behavioural intervention is effective enough to change behaviours sufficiently to reduce or alleviate the originating complaints about them, it may not be considered truly effective unless it also survives, as an intervention, as long as the problem it solves is there to be solved by it. Suppose, for example, that a teacher complains that her students are so unruly that teaching them anything is difficult, and that even when they are reasonably well behaved, they learn little. Suppose that we offer her some of the many behavioural intervention programs that solve such problems (e.g., O'Leary & O'Leary, 1972), and that with our support, she uses these interventions to achieve a classroom of well-behaved, hard-working, high-achieving students. The teacher expresses delight, and reports that her problem has been solved completely. The first meaning of effectiveness has been achieved. And so suppose further that after a year of this thorough success, we withdraw, because it is clear that she knows exactly how to continue these programmes herself, and is well able to do so. But suppose that we check this classroom two years later, and find none of the programmes being practised, and the current children once again rowdy and unaccomplished. The second meaning of effectiveness has not been achieved: some successful programmes were put in place but did not survive, even though the problems for which they are effective solutions are still present and still demanding solution, and those programmes would still solve those problems if applied to them. Then we need a doubly effective programme: one that will reduce all the teacher's complaints, and one that she will continue to use after we are gone. Put differently, we were ineffective because our initial analysis was incomplete: we analysed the children's deportment and academic achievement, but not their teacher's tolerance for the programmes that accomplish that. Thus, for effectiveness, the analysis of her tolerance is the most important next research question.

That research would go better if we could predict reliably when the people who use behaviour-change programmes in our presence will not continue using them in our absence, or when they dislike our programmes but are reluctant to say so in our presence. The interview and questionnaire techniques aimed at accomplishing that kind of prediction have been prescribed and named *social validity* (Wolf, 1978), but they have not yet been studied enough to evaluate their effectiveness for that purpose, and they are very likely still incomplete (Schwartz & Baer, 1991). The evaluation of social validity is one of the major research questions in modern practice.

Capable of generalized effects

A very frequent finding in behavioural intervention is that the target behaviours change readily enough in the setting in which the intervention takes place, but that those changes do not generalize to all the other places where those behaviour changes are desired. Thus a speech therapist will often discover that a child's poor articulation can be improved greatly through imitation and differential reinforcement with the therapist in the clinic, but that the child now articulates better only there and only in the presence of the speech therapist, and not yet with parents, friends, other teachers, and peers in other places. Modern applied behaviour analysis systematically assumes that the desired generalizations of any behaviour change will not occur naturally, and will have to be made to happen: they will require explicit programming. In 1977 Stokes and Baer reviewed what was known about techniques that could foster generalization, and found a surprising number of techniques that succeed at least sometimes (see also Drabman, Hammer, & Rosenbaum, 1979; Marholin & Siegel, 1978): teaching enough of the correct kinds of examples, teaching in a variety of places and with a variety of teachers, obscuring where and when behaviour-change procedures operate or do not, making sure that salient events in the teaching situations also occur wherever else generalization is desired, varying irrelevant aspects of the teaching situation so that they cannot inadvertently acquire inappropriate discriminative control of the new behaviour, establishing mediating rules and other forms of self-control for use in non-teaching settings, and so on.

The current flowering of that line of research is well summarized in the text, *Generalization and Maintenance*, edited by Horner, Dunlap, and Koegel (1988). Perhaps a fair summary of current knowledge and technique is that any behaviour change within the technology of behaviour change can be made to generalize as its teachers desire, if they know this auxiliary technology of generalization, and are willing to do the work that it prescribes, perhaps with some experimentation in finding the optimum technique for the problem in hand.

SUMMARY

Any clinical discipline that meets the criteria defined above, as applied, behavioural, analytic, technological, conceptually systematic, effective, and capable of generalized effects, may fairly be called applied behaviour analysis. At present, that discipline relies greatly on the reinforcement concept and its techniques. That reliance is not part of its definition, however; as more effective concepts and techniques are found − if they are − they will surely be incorporated into applied behaviour analysis, if they can meet the seven criteria; if so, they may well change its character to some extent. Applied behaviour analysis is a discipline about behaviour change whose own behaviour is open to change.

FURTHER READING

Catania, A. C. (1984). *Learning* (2nd edn). Englewood Cliffs, NJ: Prentice-Hall.
Horner, R. H., Dunlap, G., & Koegel, R. L. (Eds) (1988). *Generalization and maintenance*: *Life-style changes in applied settings*. Baltimore, MD: Paul H. Brookes.
Martin, G., & Pear, J. (1978). *Behavior modification*: *What it is and how to do it*. Englewood Cliffs, NJ: Prentice-Hall.
Reese, E. P. (with J. Howard & T. P. Reese) (1978). *Human operant behavior*: *Analysis and application* (2nd edn). Dubuque, IA: W. C. Brown.
Sulzer-Azaroff, B., & Mayer, G. R. (1991). *Behavior analysis for lasting change*. Fort Worth, TX: Holt, Rinehart & Winston.

REFERENCES

Baer, D. M. (1988). If you know why you're changing a behavior, you'll know when you've changed it enough. *Behavioral Assessment, 10*, 219–223.

Baer, D. M., Wolf, M. M., & Risley, T. R. (1968). Some current dimensions of applied behavior analysis. *Journal of Applied Behavior Analysis*, *1*, 1–7.

Baer, D. M., Wolf, M. M., & Risley, T. R. (1987). Some still-current dimensions of applied behavior analysis. *Journal of Applied Behavior Analysis*, *20*, 313–327.

Carr, E. G., & Durand, V. M. (1985). Reducing behavior problems through functional communication training. *Journal of Applied Behavior Analysis*, *18*, 111–126.

Catania, A. C. (1984). *Learning* (2nd edn). Englewood Cliffs, NJ: Prentice-Hall.

Cautela, J. R., & Wysocki, P. A. (1977). The thought stopping procedure: Description, application, and learning theory interpretations. *Psychological Record*, *27*, 255–264.

Drabman, R. S., Hammer, D., & Rosenbaum, M. S. (1979). Assessing generalization in behavior modification with children: The generalization map. *Behavioral Assessment*, *1*, 203–219.

Horner, R. H., Dunlap, G., & Koegel, R. L. (Eds) (1988). *Generalization and maintenance: Life-style changes in applied settings*. Baltimore, MD: Paul H. Brookes.

Iwata, B. A., Pace, G. M., Kalsher, M. J., Cowdery, G. E., & Cataldo, M. F. (1990). Experimental analysis and extinction of self-injurious escape behavior. *Journal of Applied Behavior Analysis*, *23*, 11–27.

Kazdin, A. E. (1977). *The token economy: A review and evaluation*. New York: Plenum.

Kazdin, A. E. (1982). *Single-case research designs: Methods for clinical and applied settings*. Oxford: Oxford University Press.

Marholin, D., & Siegel, L. J. (1978). Beyond the law of effect: Programming for the maintenance of behavior change. In D. Marholin (Ed.) *Child behavior therapy* (pp. 397–415). New York: Gardner.

Martin, G., & Pear, J. (1978). *Behavior modification: What it is and how to do it*. Englewood Cliffs, NJ: Prentice-Hall.

O'Leary, K. D., & O'Leary, S. G. (Eds) (1972). *Classroom management: The successful use of behavior modification*. New York: Pergamon.

Pinkston, E. M., Reese, N. M., LeBlanc, J. M., & Baer, D. M. (1973). Independent control of a preschooler's aggression and peer interaction by contingent teacher attention. *Journal of Applied Behavior Analysis*, *6*, 1, 323–334.

Pinkston, E. M., Levitt, J. L., Green, G. R., Linsk, N. L., & Rzepnicki, T. L. (1982). *Effective social work practice: Advanced techniques for behavioral intervention with individuals, families, and institutional staff*. San Francisco, CA: Jossey-Bass.

Reese, E. P. (with J. Howard & T. W. Reese) (1978). *Human operant behavior: Analysis and application* (2nd edn). Dubuque, IA: W. C. Brown.

Reiss, S., & Bootzin, R. R. (Eds) (1985). *Theoretical issues in behavior therapy*. New York: Academic Press.

Schwartz, I. S., & Baer, D. M. (1991). Social validity assessments: Is current practice state of the art? *Journal of Applied Behavior Analysis*, *24*, 189–204.

Skinner, B. F. (1938). *The behavior of organisms*. New York: Appleton.

Skinner, B. F. (1953). *Science and human behavior*. New York: Macmillan.

Stokes, T. F., & Baer, D. M. (1977). An implicit technology of generalization. *Journal of Applied Behavior Analysis*, *10*, 349–367.

Stubbs, D. A., & Cohen, S. L. (1972). Second-order schedules: Comparison of different procedures for scheduling paired and nonpaired brief stimuli. *Journal of the Experimental Analysis of Behavior*, *18*, 403–413.

Sulzer-Azaroff, B., & Mayer, G. R. (1991). *Behavior analysis for lasting change*. Fort Worth, TX: Holt, Rinehart & Winston.

Wilson, G. T., & Franks, C. M. (Eds) (1982). *Contemporary behavior therapy*: *Conceptual and empirical foundations*. New York: Guilford.

Wolf, M. M. (1978). Social validity: The case for subjective measurement, or how behavior analysis is finding its heart. *Journal of Applied Behavior Analysis, 11*, 203–214.

Zuriff, G. E. (1985). *Behaviorism: A conceptual reconstruction*. New York: Columbia University Press.

3

COGNITIVE SKILLS

K. Anders Ericsson
Florida State University, USA

William L. Oliver
Florida State University, USA

Acquisition of simple cognitive skills	Performance of experts on domain-specific tasks
Acquisition of cognitive skills in everyday life	Cognitive processes mediating expert performance
Expertise and expert performance	Acquisition of superior memory performance
Capturing expert performance in the laboratory	**Conclusion**
	Further reading
	References

Skill refers to superior performance that is acquired through extended practice and training. Before its use in psychology, the term was used to distinguish skilled and unskilled labour. A skilled worker had the prerequisite aptitudes to carry out complex jobs, whereas an unskilled worker was limited to perform jobs that could be mastered in relatively short times (Welford, 1968). The aptitudes required of skilled workers often involve knowledge, judgement, and manual deftness developed through years of training. The degree of skill in a domain can obviously vary, and experts and masters can be distinguished from moderately skilled performers. During the years of training to attain skilled performance, there is an incremental improvement on the many different specific tasks needed to perform the skill. Laboratory research in psychology has shied away from studying the acquisition of complex skills. Instead, laboratory research has focused on the ways in which people learn simple tasks for which large improvements can be observed within a few hours of practice.

The skills that people learn vary greatly in the relative emphasis they place on perceptual, cognitive, and motoric processes. For example, the identification of enemy aircraft at a distance would seem to reflect difficulties in perception and would be considered primarily a perceptual skill. Ballet and tight-rope walking would require the production of complex motor sequences and would be considered motor skills. The identification of cognitive skills is more difficult. This difficulty partly arises because extended practice often reduces cognitive involvement so that performance becomes automatic. Mathematicians, for instance, report that they simply "see" the correct solutions for some equations, suggesting that they first perceive and then respond directly to familiar patterns of symbols. As a working definition, *cognitive skills* can be characterized as acquired superior performance on tasks for which perception of stimuli is easy and the required motor responses are simple and part of the subjects' repertoire of responses. This definition clearly includes skill in mathematics, natural science, and other academic subjects. Skill in games, such as chess, bridge, and Go, involve perception of clearly visible configurations of pieces and cards and involve simple movements. Thus, these games meet the defining criteria for cognitive skill. Most laboratory tasks in psychology use readily perceivable stimuli and simple responses, usually button presses or vocalization of single words. Acquired superior performance on these laboratory tasks as a result of practice also qualifies them as cognitive skills.

It is important to note that skills that would *not* be classified as cognitive skills according to our definition none the less include component skills that are cognitive in nature. Skills with cognitive components include skill in sport, surgery, and artistic performance. Improvements of perceptual and motoric aspects of performance predominate in these skills, but there are clearly important cognitive aspects as well (e.g., the decisions a pianist must make on the interpretation of a piece of music). In our conclusion to this chapter we shall briefly comment on the cognitive aspects of these types of skills with cognitive components.

Much of our understanding of cognitive skills comes from the study of real-life expertise. Some insight into cognitive skills can be gained through our observation of the performance of everyday skills. Naturally occurring instances of skilled performance, however, take place in complex social and professional contexts, and it is virtually impossible to gain any general scientific knowledge about cognitive skill through mere observation. Thus, the first step towards studying cognitive skill in some domain is to identify a set of standardized tasks that can be performed in the laboratory. These standardized tasks are designed to be difficult enough to challenge the expert yet easy enough that they can be performed in brief periods of time. The tasks can then be used to elicit expert behaviour in laboratory or classroom settings so that expertise may be assessed or studied. For many academic skills, such as mathematics, there has been a long tradition in the design of test problems that can be used to measure a given individual's level of skill.

For some domains it is more difficult to identify standardized tasks that capture the essence of the real-life skill. Chess skill, for instance, is defined as the ability to defeat opponents in entire games; to measure chess skill it would seem necessary to rely on a chess rating system based on performance of players in tournament games. Fortunately, in the case of chess such a rating system is available. De Groot (1978) found that it was also possible to measure the same chess skill by having players select the best move for a series of unfamiliar chess positions. Similarly, medical skill in radiology has been assessed by testing radiologists' ability to interpret X-rays. The identification of a representative set of standardized tasks is not only important for the measurement of skill, but also necessary for the systematic study of the cognitive processes that underlie skilled performance.

An alternative approach to the study of cognitive skill looks at the acquisition of new skills in the laboratory. Practical concerns usually constrain this research to the study of simple skills that require little background knowledge and that can be acquired within relatively few hours of practice in the laboratory. Few researchers have the resources or time to study a skill that takes many years to acquire.

A comprehensive account of cognitive skill would describe skill acquisition as well as describe the knowledge and strategies used at all levels of skill including the highest international-level performance in a given domain of expertise. Most studies have been focused on some part or aspect of the skill acquisition process. We shall first discuss research on comparatively simple cognitive skills that can be attained within hours so that the entire acquisition process can be monitored in the laboratory. Then we shall review results from studies of everyday skills. Finally, we shall review research on expert performance and try to extend our framework to accommodate those findings on the highest levels of skilled performance.

ACQUISITION OF SIMPLE COGNITIVE SKILLS

Drawing on previous studies of skill acquisition, Fitts and Posner (1967) described three different acquisition stages according to a model originally proposed by Fitts. The "early or cognitive stage" involves understanding the task and its demands as well as learning what information one must attend to. During this stage an individual occasionally makes gross errors reflecting inadequate understanding. With further practice individuals move to "the intermediate and associative stage". This stage is characterized by attempts to identify efficient strategies to allow rapid perception and retrieval of required information and responses. During this stage individuals eliminate errors and increase the speed of performance. The "late or autonomous stage" involves minimizing cognitive control by making the access of correct responses automatic. During this final stage, performance is virtually error free and the speed of performance continues to improve as a result of further practice. Subsequently, Anderson (1982) provided a theoretical model with three different learning mechanisms, each corresponding to a stage of the Fitts model.

The three-stage model of skill acquisition does a remarkably good job in accounting for empirical evidence, even outside the strictly cognitive skills. The acquisition of skill in flying an airplane and telegraphy proceeds in a manner consistent with the model. For these skills, the early cognitive phase is completed within ten hours, after which major errors are rare (Fitts & Posner, 1967). Performance then becomes faster and ultimately "automatic" performance is attained.

Many laboratory tasks used to study skill acquisition are comparatively easy. After the experimenter's instruction and some practice problems, subjects understand the task and the first stage of skill acquisition is completed. An "alphabet arithmetic" task used by Compton and Logan (1991) is a good example of a laboratory task used to study skill acquisition. Subjects are shown problems like those shown in Table 1. The subjects' task is to indicate as quickly as possible whether a given letter falls n letters (given by the addend) beyond another letter in the alphabet. The subjects are to respond as quickly as possible by pressing buttons labelled "True" and "False" depending on whether a correct or incorrect answer appears on a given trial of practice. Compton and Logan found that, when generating an answer to an alphabet arithmetic problem, such as "G + 3 = ", subjects would initially report that they sequentially accessed the following three letters of the alphabet – G, H, I, J – before responding true or false. For trials with reports of sequential access, the observed reaction times increased linearly with the number of letters accessed. With practice subjects became faster and more accurate when counting off the letters (associative stage). With even more practice on the alphabet arithmetic task, subjects reported being able to access the answer directly based on past experience with the specific problems, and the observed reaction time was found to be independent of the number of letters added (autonomous stage). The primary reason for the dramatic speed-up with practice is due to an increase in the frequency of direct retrieval from memory. Consistent with the three-stage model of Fitts, generating answers in the alphabet arithmetic task starts with a fixed sequence of cognitive processes (counting off the letters) and is then transformed through practice into direct retrieval from memory. The first stage is essentially omitted because the subjects understand the task immediately and can begin practising to reduce errors and speed-up their scanning of the alphabet.

Other evidence for the three-stage model comes from research on individual differences. A number of studies have shown that tests of general

Table 1 Example problems and answers for the alphabet task with the appropriate letter sequences generated by the subjects

Problem	Letter sequence	Answer
B + 3 = E	"B–C–D–E"	True
N + 3 = R	"N–O–P–Q"	False
H + 2 = J	"H–I–J"	True

cognitive abilities, such as tests of verbal knowledge and attention efficiency, can predict which subjects will perform well and which will perform poorly when first learning a relatively complex laboratory task (Ackerman, 1987; Woltz, 1988). These same tests do not, however, predict performance level late in the acquisition process. Instead, performance differences among subjects at later stages of learning are better predicted by tests of motor or perceptual skill, depending on which of these component skills are emphasized in the task being learned. This pattern of results is consistent with the view that skill acquisition starts with a cognitive stage stressing verbal, planful processes, when subjects with verbal skills would have an advantage, and then eventually progresses to an autonomous stage stressing automatic

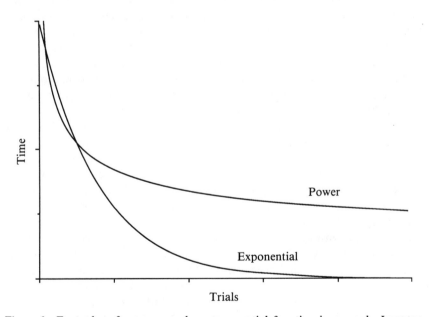

Figure 1 Examples of a power and an exponential function in a graph. Improvement curves that plot the time to perform a task as a function of trials of practice are often well described by power functions

41

responses, when subjects with efficient perceptual or motor skills would have an advantage.

Improvement during the second and third stages of skill acquisition in laboratory tasks follows very consistent patterns described mathematically by power functions (Newell & Rosenbloom, 1981). The rate of improvement, often measured by how quickly subjects can perform a task, is initially very rapid and then levels off with increasing trials of practice. Researchers have found that practice in relatively pure cognitive tasks, such as generating geometry proofs (Neves & Anderson, 1981), recognition of memorized facts (Pirolli & Anderson, 1985), and the alphabet arithmetic task (Logan, 1988) leads to improvements that follow power functions. In fact, this functional form of improvement is so consistent across task domains that one can now speak of a "power law of practice", and theories of skill acquisition are developed in part to explain why practice curves follow power functions as opposed to other functions, such as exponential functions. A power curve is contrasted with an exponential curve in Figure 1.

ACQUISITION OF COGNITIVE SKILLS IN EVERYDAY LIFE

Many cognitive skills in everyday life have been shown to develop in a way consistent with the three-stage model of skill acquisition. Most children learn to read by sounding out words, and with further practice the reading of words is converted to automatic access of the meaning of words. Children learn to generate sums by sequential counting initially using fingers, then by internalized silent counting, and finally by retrieval of familiar facts of single-digit additions. Similarly, multiplication is initially generated by sequential addition, but with instruction and training this process is replaced by direct retrieval from a memorized multiplication table.

More complex cognitive skills for solving algebra word problems and physics problems show a similar transformation with experience and practice. Beginners (novices) often have to generate their solutions step by step relying on general problem-solving methods like trial-and-error. For example, if a physics problem asks for the velocity of an object, a novice starts to retrieve formulas yielding velocity and then checks whether each formula is consistent with the given information. This method of starting with the question is called backward reasoning. In contrast, more experienced subjects (experts) proceed by forward reasoning and, as part of the comprehension of the physics problem, generate a representation of the problem which allows them to retrieve a solution plan (Simon & Simon, 1978). When experts categorize physics problems, they rely on underlying physical principles (e.g., Newton's second law and conservation of energy), whereas novices categorize problems by surface features, such as "problems involving pulleys". This finding suggests that experts form an immediate representation of problems that systematically cues their relevant knowledge, whereas novices do not have this kind of orderly efficient access to their knowledge (Chi, Glaser, & Rees, 1982).

With increased expertise in a domain, individuals accumulate more as well as better organized knowledge about that domain. With a lot of experience of algebra word problems, students recognize types of problems and can thus retrieve a solution plan from memory instead of generating the equations in step-by-step fashion (Hinsley, Hayes, & Simon, 1977). Experts in a wide range of domains, such as chess (de Groot, 1978) are able to select the appropriate action after a very brief period of exposure to a problem situation. The ability of experts to retrieve rapidly and reliably the appropriate plans and solutions from the vast body of information in long-term memory implies that the expert encodes the presented problem in terms of several patterns which, in combination, serve as memory cues (Chase & Simon, 1973).

Because improving performance of everyday skills requires learning new knowledge and strategies, the course of improvement for these skills does not always follow a trajectory implied by the three-stage model of skill acquisition or by power functions. For instance, Thorndike (1921) observed that clerks often failed to learn to add numbers faster even though they frequently performed the task. Similarly, adults' handwriting does not necessarily become faster or more legible with time. Also, the learning of skills is often very specific and does not transfer to other skills. For instance, Brazilian children who work as street vendors can perform complex calculations to ply their trade, but cannot perform similar calculations in a classroom setting (Carraher, Carraher, & Schliemann, 1985). Skills sometimes do transfer within domains or to very related domains as in the case of text editing or word processing on computers (Singley & Anderson, 1989). A text editor can be learned more quickly after one has used a different text editor because many of the goals are the same across text editors (e.g., moving a block of text), although the commands or keystrokes to achieve the goals differ.

A number of studies have examined the long-term retention of everyday, cognitive skills when the skills are no longer being used. Skills that have not been highly practised appear to be lost fairly rapidly once they are no longer used. Highly practised skills are retained very well, however, so that a student's skill at algebra that is being used in a calculus course is retained for life even though the more tenuously learned skill at calculus is rapidly lost with disuse (Bahrick & Hall, 1991).

EXPERTISE AND EXPERT PERFORMANCE

The highest levels of cognitive skills are generally referred to as expert performance. Typically, an expert is a successful, full-time professional in a domain. Domains of expertise include specialties of medicine, engineering, law as well as academic disciplines. The best individuals in competitive games, such as chess, bridge, Go, and backgammon, are also considered to be experts. The superior achievements and performance of experts are socially recognized by awards, prizes, and promotions to higher-paid jobs. Hence, there is a fair consensus on who the experts are, but the real problem is to characterize how experts differ from less accomplished people in general terms.

Being an expert in a domain, such as medicine or physics, involves superior performance on a vast number of different tasks. An analysis of any one of those tasks reveals a large body of knowledge and skill that are necessary even to be able to complete these tasks. Around 20 years of schooling is often a prerequisite for attaining the necessary knowledge and skills, which would roughly correspond to the early and cognitive phase in Fitts's framework. An additional 10 years of full-time experience is often necessary to attain expert status in the domain (Ericsson & Crutcher, 1990). The highest achievement of an expert in these domains consists of a discovery of a new technique, fact or theory that extends the accumulated knowledge in that domain. These achievements are primarily made by experts in their 30s and early 40s (Lehman, 1953).

Games, such as chess and bridge, differ from academic domains in that the necessary rules can be learned in a matter of hours. There is no prerequisite knowledge learned in schools, and children as young as 5–6 years of age can play these games. Based on the results from tournaments, it is possible to measure the level of performance for a given individual on an objective scale, such as the chess rating system. By examining biographical data on world-class chess players in the nineteenth and twentieth centuries, the time course for learning to play chess at the highest levels of skill can be charted. Simon and Chase (1973) found that all international-level chess players had spent 10 or more years in intensive study of chess before attaining their level of expertise. Outstanding chess players tend to have started playing chess at young ages (on the average between 9 and 10 years of age), and for those players that started later during adolescence, 10 years or more of chess study is still needed to achieve a high level of skill (Ericsson & Crutcher, 1990). The acquisition of chess skill of recent players achieving very high levels can be traced by examining their chess ratings as a function of age. Elo (1978) found that at age 12 these players played at the same level as average adult players. During adolescence there was a steep improvement, levelling off in the early 20s. During this period the international-level players improved more and attained a higher final level. The highest achievement of elite chess players is normally attained between 30 and 40 years of age (Elo, 1965). The parallels between acquisition of expert performance in chess and in more traditional domains of expertise, such as science and medicine, are striking and suggest intriguing commonalities. Research (Charness, 1991) has detailed the vast amount of knowledge about chess – for example, the many thousands of variants of chess openings – that expert chess players know.

Capturing expert performance in the laboratory

A central problem in all research on expert performance is that real-life expertise occurs in complex and highly interactive situations. A medical expert diagnosing the disease of a patient engages in an extended interview with the patient, often requiring subsequent medical tests and physical examinations. The chess games played by chess experts last several hours, and each game is different from all of the tens of thousands of other chess games that the chess expert has previously played in his or her life. Hence, a given expert will most likely never play the same chess game twice in his or her life, nor are two different experts ever likely to encounter identical middle-game chess positions. This problem of not being able to observe many experts (as well as novices) in the same situation is a major challenge for research on real-life expertise.

The general solution to this problem is to analyse carefully the real-life expertise to identify brief segments of the experts' behaviour that capture the essence of the naturally occurring task. The researcher then studies these brief segments of behaviour under various experimental conditions to gain insight into the expertise. For example, a chess expert has to select the next move for the current chess position. Due to the wide range of different chess positions that can occur during games with many different opponents, it is reasonable to assume that a stronger chess player would be able to select a better move (on the average) than a weaker chess player. Research (Charness, 1981; de Groot, 1978) has shown that the ability of chess players to select good moves for chess positions is strongly correlated with the standard chess ratings from actual chess tournaments. Thus, research on chess skill has examined the ability of chess experts to generate good moves for selected positions (e.g., under speed conditions) with the confidence that an important component of chess expertise is captured by the task. Similarly, it is possible to present a medical expert with a summary of relevant information about a patient to capture the cognitive processes of diagnosing the patient's disease. This situation would occur naturally when a doctor asks a colleague for help in diagnosing a difficult case. Laboratory studies show that the accuracy of diagnosis increases with the level of medical expertise (Patel & Groen, 1991).

Performance of experts on domain-specific tasks

Research comparing the performance of individuals at different levels of expertise shows that experts select the correct action for representative tasks, whereas less accomplished individuals select inferior or incorrect actions. This important finding implies that the mediating cognitive processes are qualitatively different at different levels of expertise, in contrast to the earlier discussed simpler cognitive skills where the primary differences concerned the speed of generating correct responses. In other words, experts may differ from novices by focusing on different information or by using altogether different strategies to perform a task, and therefore *cannot* be thought of as carrying out the same mental steps as novices in faster and more efficient ways. Another important implication is that improved accuracy of performance cannot be attained by simply doing the same thing again and again. To attain more accurate performance subjects need to change their cognitive processes by learning to allow generation of the correct responses on a subsequent occasion. Consistent with the need for continuous learning in the acquisition of expert performance, the number of years of experience with a domain has often only a relatively weak correlation with actual performance.

In some domains of expertise investigators have been unable to identify superior performance of "experts". Often these domains involve decision-making and forecasting of complex economic, social, and medical events, where the lack of immediate feedback and the probabilistic nature of these events would make learning slow and difficult (Camerer & Johnson, 1991). In many other domains, such as surgery, internal medicine, and academic skill, experts display reliable superior performance on tasks representative of their domain. The performance of these experts can be studied to identify the cognitive processes that underlie their expertise.

Cognitive processes mediating expert performance

There are many types of observations that can be collected on subjects' cognitive processes while they generate their response to a representative task (Ericsson & Oliver, 1988). The most important technique involves instructing subjects to verbalize their thoughts concurrently (think aloud), but subjects can also be asked to recall their thoughts retrospectively once the task is completed.

Comparisons between think-aloud protocols of novices and experts often reveal qualitative differences in the cognitive processes. Studies comparing novice and expert writers show particularly striking differences in their strategies. Novice writers tend to write down ideas on topics as they occur to them, whereas expert writers spend a lot of time planning their text to fit the particular audience and meet the appropriate goals of the genre (Scardemalia & Bereiter, 1991). This planning results in expert writers taking much longer to write texts than novice writers. The texts produced by the experts, however, are qualitatively superior to those of the novices. Medical doctors and students at different levels of expertise differ in their ability to diagnose a disease from a description of a patient. In addition to the experts' more reliable access to and better integration of their knowledge about diseases (Feltovich, Johnson, Moller, & Swanson, 1984), the medical experts were better able to integrate information about the patient and discover inconsistencies. They could also recover more easily from incorrect diagnostic hypotheses they had generated earlier. Patel and Groen (1986) have shown that after a brief review of the patient chart, the medical expert is able not only to recall the relevant information but also to give an integrated account of the underlying pathophysiology of the case. Experts store the relevant information about a case in a well-integrated representation in long-term memory, and their recall of this information is superior to lesser experts when given unexpected tests of memory (Norman, Brooks, & Allen, 1989).

Cognitive processes mediating the selection of chess moves for a given position have been extensively studied and related to expertise in chess. Chess players at all levels of expertise spend several minutes considering alternative moves and mentally exploring the consequences of potential moves by planning. The number of moves chess players plan ahead depends on their level of chess skill (Charness, 1989). The planning and evaluation of consequences of potential chess moves is critical even for international chess masters. Even though a chess master can retrieve several promising moves within seconds of seeing the chess position, systematic planning is necessary to select the best move or occasionally to discover an even better move (de Groot, 1978). Being able to mentally represent the chess position after a sequence of conceived chess moves requires superior memory for chess positions.

Early research in the 1920s showed that chess masters have superior memory for chess positions, but their memory for other types of information was in the normal range. De Groot (1978) found that chess experts could recall the location of most chess pieces after having selected a chess move for a position, and that the amount of recall was related to the level of chess expertise of the subject. In their classic research, Chase and Simon (1973) systematically studied intentional memory for briefly presented chess positions (see the top panel of Figure 2) as well as chess boards with randomly arranged pieces (see the bottom panel of Figure 2). The amount of recall for chess positions increased with chess expertise and the chess master was able to recall the locations of many pieces for chess positions from normal games. However, the recall for random boards was uniformly low (around four pieces) regardless of chess expertise. Chase and Simon argued that chess experts recognize familiar patterns, for example, strings of pawns, in the normal board positions. These patterns are stored in short-term memory, as larger patterns or chunks of information. Both chess experts and novices had difficulty remembering the random boards because few familiar chess patterns could be identified and those patterns that appeared by chance did not form a coherent, larger pattern corresponding to a normal chess board position. Subsequent research has shown that the chess masters' superior memory for chess positions reflects storage in long-term memory (Charness, 1991). In many other types of expert performance, experts show superior memory for information from their domains of expertise (Ericsson & Staszewski, 1989). Expert memory aids in planning, reasoning, and the storage of information

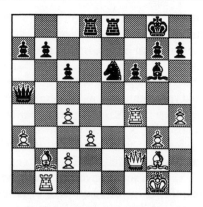

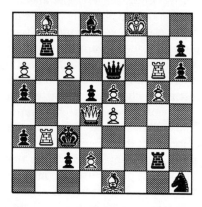

Figure 2 An example of a normal chess board position appears at the top of the figure. A random configuration of the same pieces appears in the board position at the bottom of the figure

in temporary states, such as when experts solve complex physics problems. Insight into how superior memory for a specific domain can be attained is best provided by research on the acquisition of memory skill in the laboratory.

Acquisition of superior memory performance

Improvements in performance on a memory task as function of practice is a cognitive skill and has been studied directly. Chase and Ericsson (1981, 1982) arranged for a college student (SF) to practise on a digit-span task in which subjects must recall a list of digits that is rapidly presented (1 digit/second). The digits must be recalled in their presented order without any errors. During the first practice sessions SF rehearsed the digits to himself and was able to reproduce lists of about seven digits. His initial performance was typical for untrained college students in this task. With practice on the task SF's performance improved steadily (see Figure 3). As shown in the figure, SF is not alone in his ability to recall long digit strings. The subject DD eventually acquired a digit span over 100 digits after over 800 practice sessions (Staszewski, 1988)!

SF's superior memory performance was possible only after qualitative changes in his cognitive processes compared to his initial use of rehearsal to recall the presented digits. Initially, SF reported segmenting the list of presented digits into groups, e.g., 7 digits would be 3 + 4 digits (like a telephone number). During the fifth session SF came up with the idea of encoding digit groups as running times with a dramatic increase in his performance as a result. SF was an experienced runner and knew a lot about running times for different races. For example 352 could be encoded as 3 minutes and 52 seconds and a near world-record time for the mile. Encoding digit groups as running times augmented by numerical patterns allowed SF to think briefly about a given digit group before considering the next digit group. For longer digit strings, SF adopted the strategy of deciding ahead of time how to segment the numbers. For example, 13 digits would be segmented into three 3-digit groups and a single 4-digit group. As SF improved

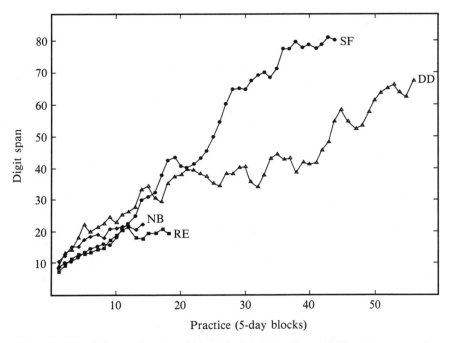

Figure 3 The digit span for four subjects is shown as a function of one-hour practice sessions averaged over blocks of five sessions

further, he invented hierarchical structures. For example, a given digit might fall in the second digit group in the last portion (third portion) of the list. At recall he could then regenerate locations in the list as retrieval cues to recall the associated digit groups. The period of arrests in improvement in Figure 3 were associated with problem-solving efforts in extending his retrieval structures to allow reliable retrieval of additional digit groups. SF's acquisition of his memory skill should be seen as successive reorganization of his cognitive processes in line with our general claims about expert performance.

Based on the evidence from SF and the other trained subjects as well as from other individuals with exceptional memory, Chase and Ericsson (1982) proposed a theory of skilled memory. According to skilled-memory theory, superior and exceptional memory reflect acquired ability to store information in LTM in retrievable form. Rapid storage of information in memory requires a body of associated knowledge and patterns. For example, SF relied on running times and other subjects rely on their knowledge of numbers. Information is associated to a retrieval structure at the time of encoding, which allows efficient retrieval at recall. All memory skills are domain-specific and show essentially no transfer to other materials due to the specificity of the encoding processes. For example, when SF's digit-span had increased by over 1,000 per cent, his memory span for consonants remained at only six letters.

Skilled-memory theory has been extended to account for the superior domain-specific memory of experts (Ericsson & Staszewski, 1989). A review of the superior memory of experts shows that it is not an inevitable consequence of expertise, as experts in some domain do not display it (Ericsson & Pennington, 1993). Instead, superior memory in a domain is related to the demands for extended working memory to support planning and reasoning. Superior memory requires the acquisition of encoding processes and retrieval structures uniquely tailored to meet the demands on memory in that domain.

In sum, our characterization of the acquisition of expert performance is not consistent with a linear progression through Fitts's three stages of skills. Instead experts continue to return to the early cognitive phase to improve their understanding of the task and to uncover superior methods and new knowledge to further increase the accuracy of their performance. In many instances, experts develop memory skills to overcome limits on short-term memory so that they can more effectively plan and reason. This continuous restructuring and refinement of the mediating processes by experts implies that doing the same thing over and over (mere repetition) will not lead to expert performance. In support of this claim we noted earlier that the level of performance is often weakly correlated with the amount of experience in that domain. Instead, the attained level of performance in a domain appears to be closely correlated with the amount of time spent deliberately trying to improve one's performance (deliberate practice) (Ericsson, Krampe, &

Tesch-Römer, 1993). For example, chess experts do not rely on simply playing many games to improve; in addition to playing games, they spend up to four hours a day studying published games of international chess masters. Failure to predict a move made by the master in a studied chess game provides an opportunity to analyse the chess position more carefully. Similarly, medical practitioners regularly discuss the diagnosis and treatment of their patients with their colleagues and with their supervising head of the clinic at weekly case conferences. For virtually any domain of expertise there exists deliberate practice activities that maximize opportunities for learning and improvement.

CONCLUSION

Cognitive skill refers to the greatly improved performance on cognitive tasks as a result of practice. The acquisition of simple cognitive skills is well described by Fitts's three-phase model, where the task is first understood (cognitive phase) then responses are learned (associative phase) and finally these responses become directly retrievable (autonomous phase). In these simple tasks, performance becomes accurate relatively soon after practice begins and the speed to perform the task increases as a function of the number of practice trials. Many cognitive skills in everyday life are acquired in a similar manner. In contrast, performance of experts in more complex domains is acquired over many years of training with steadily improved accuracy. The cognitive processes mediating expert performance are continually revised to accommodate new knowledge and better methods to perform the tasks, which include the acquisition of memory skills to support the memory-demanding activities of planning and reasoning. As a result of deliberate efforts to improve their performance, experts acquire strategies and skills that differ qualitatively from the strategies and skills of novices. The changes in strategies and the acquisition of skills to overcome basic information-processing complicate efforts to predict expert level of performance from the individual differences of beginners. The success of such prediction has been found to be surprisingly poor – accounting only for 1–4 per cent of the variance (Ghiselli, 1966).

So far our review has been limited to cognitive skills. Research on typing and expert performance in sports shows the central importance of cognitive factors. Comparisons of typists at different level of expert performance show that the best typists look further ahead of the letters currently being typed. When preview of the text to be typed is eliminated in an experimental condition, the experts' typing speed is reduced to the level of novices (Salthouse, 1991). The experts are able to attain their high typing speed to a great extent by preparing for future key strokes in advance. Similarly, expert tennis players can return hard tennis serves because they learn to perceive their opponents' preparatory movements prior to the actual hitting of the tennis ball (Abernethy, 1991). Through the acquisition of anticipatory processing strategies, experts in motor skills can circumvent the limits imposed by simple serial reaction time. Expert athletes in team sports, such as basketball and field hockey, display superior memory for briefly presented pictures of game situations, but not for random arrangements of players (Allard & Starkes, 1991). The ability to correctly represent a game situation is essential for the quick selection of correct current actions and the preparation for future actions and events. Similarly, research on perceptual skills has shown the importance of cognitive factors. For instance, research has revealed the cognitive strategies used to perform seemingly pure perceptual tasks, such as determining the sex of a chicken (Biederman & Shiffrar, 1987) and identification of different shades of a colour or different pitches of tones (Ericsson & Faivre, 1988). Subjects have been able to use these strategies to develop absolute pitch, an ability that many have viewed as innate. A wide range of exceptional performance has been analysed and successful accounts in terms of acquired skill has been given (Howe, 1990).

Studies of cognitive skill and expert performance have shown that effective methods and strategies allow individuals to attain high levels of performance and circumvent basic processing limits. Further research on cognitive skill is likely to play an important role in advancing our knowledge about human cognition.

FURTHER READING

Chi, M. T. H., Glaser, R., & Farr, M. J. (Eds) (1988). *The nature of expertise*. Hillsdale, NJ: Lawrence Erlbaum.

Colley, A. M., & Beech, J. R. (Eds) (1989). *Acquisition and performance of cognitive skills*. New York: Wiley.

Ericsson, K. A., & Smith, J. (Eds) (1991). *Toward a general theory of expertise*: *Prospects and limits*. Cambridge: Cambridge University Press.

VanLehn, K. (1989). Problem solving and cognitive skill acquisition. In M. I. Posner (Ed.) *Foundations of cognitive science* (pp. 527–580). Cambridge, MA: Massachusetts Institute of Technology Press.

REFERENCES

Abernethy, B. (1991). Visual search strategies and decision-making in sport. *International Journal of Sport Psychology*, *22*, 189–210.

Ackerman, P. L. (1987). Individual differences in skill learning: An integration of psychometric and information processing perspectives. *Psychological Bulletin*, *102*, 3–27.

Allard, F., & Starkes, J. L. (1991). Motor-skill experts in sports, dance and other domains. In K. A. Ericsson & J. Smith (Eds) *Toward a general theory of expertise: Prospects and limits* (pp. 126–152). Cambridge: Cambridge University Press.

Anderson, J. R. (1982). Acquisition of cognitive skill. *Psychological Review*, *89*, 369–406.

Bahrick, H. P., & Hall, L. K. (1991). Lifetime maintenance of high school mathematics content. *Journal of Experimental Psychology: General*, *120*, 20–33.

Biederman, I., & Shiffrar, M. (1987). Sexing day-old chicks: A case study and expert systems analysis of a difficult perceptual-learning task. *Journal of Experimental Psychology: Learning, Memory & Cognition*, *13*, 640–645.

Camerer, C. F., & Johnson, E. J. (1991). The process-performance paradox in expert judgment: How can the experts know so much and predict so badly? In K. A. Ericsson & J. Smith (Eds) *Toward a general theory of expertise: Prospects and limits* (pp. 195–217). Cambridge: Cambridge University Press.

Carraher, T. N., Carraher, D. W., & Schliemann, A. D. (1985). Mathematics in the streets and in the schools. *British Journal of Developmental Psychology*, *3*, 21–29.

Charness, N. (1981). Search in chess: Age and skill differences. *Journal of Experimental Psychology: Human Perception and Performance*, *7*, 467–476.

Charness, N. (1989). Expertise in chess and bridge. In D. Klahr & K. Kotovsky (Eds) *Complex information processing: The impact of Herbert A. Simon* (pp. 183–208). Hillsdale, NJ: Lawrence Erlbaum.

Charness, N. (1991). Expertise in chess: The balance between knowledge and search. In K. A. Ericsson & J. Smith (Eds) *Toward a general theory of expertise: Prospects and limits* (pp. 39–63). Cambridge: Cambridge University Press.

Chase, W. G., & Ericsson, K. A. (1981). Skilled memory. In J. R. Anderson (Ed.) *Cognitive skills and their acquisition* (pp. 141–189). Hillsdale, NJ: Lawrence Erlbaum.

Chase, W. G., & Ericsson, K. A. (1982). Skill and working memory. In G. H. Bower (Ed.) *The psychology of learning and motivation* (vol. 16, pp. 1–58). New York: Academic Press.

Chase, W. G., & Simon, H. A. (1973). The mind's eye in chess. In W. G. Chase (Ed.) *Visual information processing* (pp. 215–281). New York: Academic Press.

Chi, M. T. H., Glaser, R., & Rees, E. (1982). Expertise in problem solving. In R. J. Sternberg (Ed.) *Advances in the psychology of human intelligence* (vol. 1, pp. 1–75). Hillsdale, NJ: Lawrence Erlbaum.

Compton, B. J., & Logan, G. D. (1991). The transition from algorithm to retrieval in memory-based theories of automaticity. *Memory & Cognition*, *19*(2), 151–158.

de Groot, A. (1978). *Thought and choice and chess*. The Hague: Mouton (original work published 1946).

Elo, A. E. (1965). Age changes in master chess performance. *Journal of Gerontology*, *20*, 289–299.

Elo, A. E. (1978). *The rating of chessplayers, past and present*. London: Batsford.

Ericsson, K. A., & Crutcher, R. J. (1990). The nature of exceptional performance. In P. B. Baltes, D. L. Featherman, & R. M. Lerner (Eds) *Life-span development and behavior* (vol. 10, pp. 187–217). Hillsdale, NJ: Lawrence Erlbaum.

Ericsson, K. A., & Faivre, I. A. (1988). What's exceptional about exceptional abilities? In I. K. Obler & D. Fein (Eds) *The exceptional brain: Neuropsychology of talent and special abilities* (pp. 436–473). New York: Guilford.

Ericsson, K. A., & Oliver, W. L. (1988). Methodology for laboratory research on thinking: Task selection, collection of observation and data analysis. In R. J. Sternberg and E. E. Smith (Eds) *The psychology of human thought* (pp. 392–428). Cambridge: Cambridge University Press.

Ericsson, K. A., & Pennington, N. (1993). Experts and expertise. In G. Davis & R. Logie (Eds) *Memory in everyday life*. Amsterdam: North Holland.

Ericsson, K. A., & Smith, J. (1991). Prospects and limits in the empirical study of expertise: An introduction. In K. A. Ericsson & J. Smith (Eds) *Toward a general theory of expertise: Prospects and limits* (pp. 1–38). Cambridge: Cambridge University Press.

Ericsson, K. A., & Staszewski, J. J. (1989). Skilled memory and expertise: Mechanisms of exceptional performance. In D. Klahr & K. Kotovsky (Eds) *Complex information processing: The impact of Herbert A. Simon* (pp. 235–267). Hillsdale, NJ: Lawrence Erlbaum.

Ericsson, K. A., Krampe, R., & Tesch-Römer, C. (1993). The role of deliberate practice in the acquisition of expert performance. *Psychological Review, 100*, 363–406.

Feltovich, P. J., Johnson, P. E., Moller, J. H., & Swanson, D. B. (1984). LCS: The role and development of medical knowledge in diagnostic expertise. In W. J. Clancey & E. H. Shortliffe (Eds) *Readings in medical artificial intelligence* (pp. 275–319). Reading, MA: Addison-Wesley.

Fitts, P. M., & Posner, M. I. (1967). *Human performance.* Belmont, CA: Brooks/Cole.

Ghiselli, E. (1966). *The validity of occupational aptitude tests.* New York: Wiley.

Hinsley, D. A., Hayes, J. R., & Simon, H. A. (1977). From words to equations: Meaning and representation in algebra word problem. In M. A. Just & P. A. Carpenter (Eds) *Cognitive processes in comprehension* (pp. 89–106). Hillsdale, NJ: Lawrence Erlbaum.

Howe, M. J. A. (1990). *The origins of exceptional abilities.* Oxford: Basil Blackwell.

Lehman, H. C. (1953). *Age and achievement.* Princeton, NJ: Princeton University Press.

Logan, G. D. (1988). Toward an instance theory of automatization. *Psychological Review, 95*, 492–527.

Neves, D. M., & Anderson, J. R. (1981). Knowledge compilation: Mechanisms for the automatization of cognitive skills. In J. R. Anderson (Ed.) *Cognitive skills and their acquisition* (pp. 57–84). Hillsdale, NJ: Lawrence Erlbaum.

Newell, A., & Rosenbloom, P. S. (1981). Mechanisms of skill acquisition and the law of practice. In J. R. Anderson (Ed.) *Cognitive skills and their acquisition* (pp. 1–55). Hillsdale, NJ: Lawrence Erlbaum.

Norman, G. R., Brooks, L. R., & Allen, S. W. (1989). Recall by expert medical practitioners and novices as a record of processing attention. *Journal of Experimental Psychology: Learning, Memory and Cognition, 15*, 1166–1174.

Patel, V. L., & Groen, G. L. (1986). Knowledge based solution strategies in medical reasoning. *Cognitive Science, 10*, 91–116.

Patel, V. L., & Groen, G. J. (1991). The general and specific nature of medical expertise: A critical look. In K. A. Ericsson & J. Smith (Eds) *Toward a general theory of expertise: Prospects and limits* (pp. 93–125). Cambridge: Cambridge University Press.

Pirolli, P., & Anderson, J. R. (1985). The role of practice in fact retrieval. *Journal of Psychology: Learning, Memory, and Cognition, 11*, 136–153.

Salthouse, T. A. (1991). Expertise as the circumvention of human processing limitations. In K. A. Ericsson & J. Smith (Eds) *Toward a general theory of expertise: Prospects and limits* (pp. 286–300). Cambridge: Cambridge University Press.

Scardemalia, M., & Bereiter, C. (1991). Literate expertise. In K. A. Ericsson & J. Smith (Eds) *Toward a general theory of expertise: Prospects and limits* (pp. 172–194). Cambridge: Cambridge University Press.

Simon, D. P., & Simon, H. A. (1978). Individual differences in solving physics problems. In R. S. Siegler (Ed.) *Children's thinking: What develops?* (pp. 325–348). Hillsdale, NJ: Lawrence Erlbaum.

Simon, H. A., & Chase, W. G. (1973). Skill in chess. *American Scientist, 61,* 394–403.

Singley, M. K., & Anderson, J. R. (1989). *The transfer of cognitive skill.* Cambridge, MA: Harvard University Press.

Staszewski, J. J. (1988). The psychological reality of retrieval structures: An investigation of expert knowledge (doctoral dissertation, Cornell University, 1987). *Dissertation Abstracts International, 48,* 2126B.

Thorndike, E. L. (1921). *The psychology of learning,* vol. II. New York: Teachers College, Columbia University.

Welford, A. T. (1968). *Fundamentals of skill.* London: Methuen.

Woltz, D. J. (1988). An investigation of the role of working memory in procedural skill acquisition. *Journal of Experimental Psychology: General, 117,* 319–331.

4

MOTOR SKILLS

John Annett
University of Warwick, England

The problem of motor control	The acquisition of skills
The neural basis of motor control	Mechanisms of learning
Motor consistency and variability	Cognitive processes
	Verbal instruction
Motor programs	Knowledge of results
Feedback control	**Retention and transfer**
Complex skills and control hierarchies	Motor memory
	Transfer of training
Serial organization and control	**Conclusion**
	Further reading
	References

Skills occur in great variety, from those involving the whole body in sports like gymnastics, to hand skills used in everyday activities such as using hand tools and playing musical instruments, and intellectual skills such as playing chess or controlling a nuclear power station. Whatever the nature of the activity, behaviour is called *skilled*, or *a skill*, when it is (1) directed towards the attainment of an identifiable goal (for example catching the ball), and (2) so organized that the goal is reliably achieved with economy of time and effort (that is, most catches are held), and (3) has been acquired by training and practice (practice makes perfect). Obviously the topic of skill embraces a very wide range of questions in theoretical and applied psychology. The characteristics and limits of human skilled performance have been of interest to applied psychologists since the beginning of the twentieth century with early studies of morse telegraphy and typing and later of flying skills. More recently, sports psychologists have provided many detailed studies of physical skills. There have been significant advances in the understanding of the neural mechanisms underlying movement, and neurological disorders with motor implications in children (cerebral palsy) and elderly people (stroke and Parkinson's disease) have stimulated interest in assessment and rehabilitation.

To begin to understand any skill it is necessary first to consider three aspects of the problem. First, different skills employ different *effector systems*, that is, functional units of the central nervous system (CNS) connected with various groups of muscles. Second, since skills are by definition goal-directed, there is always an *object*, often some environmental variable, which is manipulated or changed by the operation of the effectors. Third, the particular way in which the effector system acts on the object to achieve the goal state is mediated by a *control system*.

Research on motor skills has given pride of place to the hand as the effector system for manipulative and control skills and, of course, the trunk and limbs are the principal effectors in whole body skills. However, other important effectors include the ocular-motor (eye-movement) system, which is involved in spatially oriented behaviour, and the vocal system, which produces some of the most highly skilled behaviour of which humans are capable. These varied effector systems have different physical properties which must be taken into account in any theoretical analysis of control mechanisms. The skeletal effectors are essentially lever systems in which the angle at the joint is controlled by balanced groups of muscles, the agonists and antagonists. As mechanical systems they have properties of mass and elasticity, which place important limitations on the movements that are physically possible and especially on the speed with which a change of joint angle can take place. But these physical properties can also be exploited in the interest of economy of both physical and computational effort. The eye, by contrast, has low inertia which enables it to make fast saccades to preselected locations, an essential requirement for spatially directed behaviour. The vocal system, which includes the muscles of the diaphragm, larynx, jaw, tongue, and lips, requires very precise integration and timing of movement sequences for the generation of speech. It is, of course, not only the muscles that are controlled but also speech sounds; hence, speech is highly dependent on auditory feedback as shown by its susceptibility to disturbances, especially delay of only a few hundred milliseconds which can induce stuttering.

The second aspect of skill, the properties of objects that are controlled, is also significant in determining the kind of control that is needed. For instance, an ordinary bicycle ridden at reasonable speed is quite stable, and all the rider has to do is control direction and forward speed. Clearly, the physical properties of the object being controlled have profound consequences for the mechanism by which control is exerted.

Control systems may, in general, be of two kinds, characterized as *feedforward* and *feedback*. In a feedforward system, output, that is, muscular activity, is controlled by a program or set of stored instructions that are initiated by a starting signal in much the same way as a domestic washing machine runs through a sequence of actions when a particular program is set up and initiated. In a feedback system a target value for one or more variables is set (often known as the set point) and output is controlled by a signal proportional to the difference between the currently sensed value and the set point. A thermostat-controlled domestic heating system is a familiar example of feedback control.

THE PROBLEM OF MOTOR CONTROL

The central issue for research on skill is how the effector mechanisms are successfully brought to bear on objects in the environment in order to fulfil the goals of the organism. The information processing analysis of human skill, current from the 1950s, although providing a very significant advance on the conditioned reflex models of the 1930s and 1940s, has turned out to be not entirely satisfactory as an account of skill. In the basic model, sensory information is seen flowing through a channel, being filtered by attentional mechanisms, stored in temporary buffers, and processed or transformed by central mechanisms into a motor output. This model followed the classic traditions of Helmholtz, Donders, and Wundt, who used the principle of subtraction to deduce the time course of a sequence of hypothesized internal processes, or black boxes (see Woodworth, 1938, chap. 14).

For example, the time required to make a decision between two courses of action can be determined by subtracting reaction time to a predictable stimulus (simple reaction time) from the time required to respond to one of two possible signals (choice reaction time). This subtraction logic was pursued vigorously and with increasing degrees of sophistication for 100 years in the search for a detailed account of the "black boxes". An important analysis by Hick (1952) showed that reaction time was proportional to stimulus information, analogous to the rate at which physical communication channels can transmit information. Limitations to skilled performance were attributed principally to the capacity of the central channel, and theorizing centred on the results of experiments on serial and choice reaction time, divided attention, and performing two tasks at once. The capacity problem was not satisfactorily resolved within the framework of a static, linear model, and later interpretations of the nature of motor control (Abernethy & Sparrow, 1992) led to the consideration of rather different questions.

The neural basis of motor control

The pathways between sensory input and motor output are neither anatomically nor functionally linear and sequential. Figure 1 (after Brooks, 1986) shows the principal neural pathways involved in voluntary movement. A number of different structures intervene between the senses and the muscles and there is a great deal of interaction between them. Information flows out from the cortex and other parts of the brain to the effectors and also back again to the "higher centres". Figure 1 suggests that intentions or goals, driven originally by the motivational (limbic) system, are formulated in the association cortex, and developed into plans, principally in the frontal lobes. The formulation of a detailed executive program to achieve a goal that requires a postural adjustment must relate bodily equilibrium to the direction and force of the intended action and here structures such as the basal ganglia, thalamus, and lateral cerebellum make essential contributions by preparatory adjustments of muscular tone and by relating muscular forces to externally perceived space. The pyramidal cells of the primary motor cortex make synaptic connections direct to the motor neurons in the spinal cord but there are

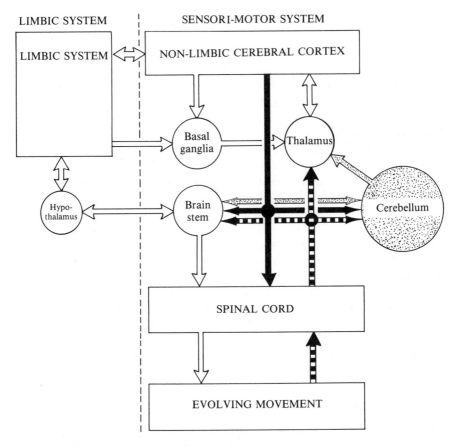

Figure 1 Principal neural pathways involved in voluntary movement
Source: After Brooks, 1986

other direct connections from the brain stem (red nucleus), and furthermore, the motor cortex interacts with the intermediate cerebellum to relate efferent signals to the changing state of sensory information. At the spinal level, both descending systems (cortico- and rubro-spinal tracts) modulate semi-autonomous spinal reflexes that control the relationships between sets of muscles. The rate and extent to which muscles change their length is dependent on a number of factors including their starting position and load and the state of other muscles that are functionally related to them or form a *synergy* or *coordinative structure* (Bernstein, 1967). The messages coming down from the brain have been likened to advice rather than instructions, since the influence of local conditions at the periphery can be strong and the relevant information may not be directly available to the higher centres. However, it is the behavioural evidence as much as the complexity of the physical mechanisms that demands a more sophisticated theory of motor control.

Motor consistency and variability

Highly skilled acts are characterized more by the constancy of their output or results than by the consistency of the muscular contractions used to achieve them. Whenever I aim to hit the *t* on my keyboard my hand comes at it from a slightly different angle, and I can pick up my coffee without first having to adopt precisely the same posture I used last time. A motor control system that depended on a centralized command structure would not be the most effective way of achieving constant goals under varying conditions. A complex joint like the shoulder is controlled by at least ten muscles, each containing a large number of motor units, that is, bundles of fibres controlled by a single nerve ending. If movements were centrally coded in terms of joint angles, then the message specifying a new position of the upper arm would require the specification of ten different values or the control of ten degrees of freedom, to use the phrase of Bernstein (1967). A moderately complex movement involving just the arms, hand, and fingers already involves a formidable number of degrees of freedom that would have to be specified in any centrally computed program. A robotics engineer designing a machine to mimic human action would look for a simpler solution, and debates in the motor skills field relate to proposed solutions. Possible solutions can be divided into those requiring stored information (feedforward models) and those that attribute action to the patterns of external stimulation and the physical properties of the responding system. Fully feedback systems are limited to relatively slow actions due to an unavoidable minimum lag time of about 100 milliseconds associated with sensory feedback.

Motor programs

Simple positioning tasks such as placing a peg in a hole (Fitts, 1954) illustrate two types of control in one movement, a pre-programmed, ballistic or open-loop initial phase followed by a controlled or closed-loop second phase. The pre-programmed phase has been taken as evidence for a general mode of feedforward control by means of a *motor program*. Different authors have slightly different conceptions of the nature of motor programs (see Summers, 1989), but the core idea is of a pattern of motor impulses which may be computed on demand or may be drawn from a memory bank. A motor program for throwing a dart into the bullseye would constitute a pattern of arm acceleration and deceleration with the finger-thumb release being timed for a particular point in the cycle.

Evidence for the existence of motor programs comes from three main sources: first, the degree to which it is possible to modify movement patterns that are subject to unforeseen mechanical forces or new information shortly after initiation; second, the effects of feedback deprivation on the execution of the motor task; and third, the relationship between initiation time and the complexity of a prepared sequence of movements. As an instance of the first type of evidence, Wadman, Denier, van der Gon, Geuze, and Moll (1979) recorded the EMG (electromyogram) signals indicating changes in the electrical potential of the muscles associated with the acceleration/deceleration pattern of a rapid sequence of arm movements. The original pattern of muscle electrical activity was preserved even on trials when the arm was unexpectedly prevented from moving strongly, suggesting pre-programmed control.

As regards feedback deprivation, Lashley (1917) noted that a patient who, due to a spinal injury, had no kinaesthetic sensation (that is, no sensation of movement) in his lower limbs could none the less reproduce movements accurately. He argued this would be possible only if there were a central memory for the motor command. Motor programs are implicated in the control of eye movements. When a pattern of excitation sweeps across the retina, the organism needs to know whether this is a result of movement in the external world or of the organism itself. A copy of the original motor instruction, an efference copy, could be used to detect the difference between self-generated and externally generated visual movement. Experiments on the accuracy of movement in the absence of sensory feedback due to surgical intervention or temporary ischaemia (Laszlo, 1966) provide supportive evidence for motor program theory to the extent that simple reaching movements can still be made in the absence of kinaesthetic feedback. However, fine control is typically lost and there are many more actions in which transformations of external sensory feedback such as delays and geometric transformations seriously disrupt performance.

It has been found that the time to produce the first response in a pre-programmed sequence increases as a linear function of the total length of the sequence. The increased reaction time is taken to reflect the time taken to retrieve the program elements from memory. This would fit with a hierarchical structure for the components of a rapid sequence of finger movements and demonstrates a linear increase in reaction time with the number of nodes in the response hierarchy that would have to be activated to produce the sequence.

Critics of the motor program concept have argued that the amount of information that would have to be retained in memory to specify all the movements of which an adult is capable would exceed the storage capacity of the brain. However, the extent of the problem may have been overestimated. Vredenbregt and Koster (1971) were able to simulate cursive handwriting by using two DC motors to drive a pen across the writing surface. Carefully timed discrete voltage pulses to the motors moving the pen in the horizontal and vertical directions produced recognizable letters due to the natural dynamics (inertia and viscosity) of the mechanical system; in other words, the information needed to specify the response is perhaps not as large as appears at first sight.

Some theories of motor control stress the role of peripheral factors, for example a limb can be considered as a mass-spring system. The angle adopted by a joint depends on the relative tension in the agonist and antagonist muscles which themselves are elastic or spring-like. It has been suggested (e.g., Bizzi, 1980) that the angle of a joint, and hence the position of a limb, can be specified in terms of the relative tension of the opposing muscles. If the initial position of the limb is disturbed by a temporary load, then it will automatically return to its former position when the load is released just as a swing door will return to its closed position after being pushed open. Muscular tension in turn can be determined by the rate of firing of the neurons serving the opposing muscle groups. The particular significance of this solution is that external disturbances caused by sudden changes of load (for instance, by hitting a small object) do not affect the final position and do not require additional processing in the nervous system. The terminal position of limb in space can also be determined by the relative tension of the opposing muscles.

Feedback control

It would be wrong to regard motor programs and feedback as mutually exclusive accounts of motor control. Actions require both some degree of preplanning and some means of monitoring and adjusting the plan if the intended results are to be achieved under variable conditions. The operation of the feedback principle in the central nervous system (CNS) was noted by Bell as long ago as the 1820s (Bell, 1826), but it is only since the 1940s following the work of Craik and others (Craik, 1947) at Cambridge on the skills of pilots and gun layers that its significance for motor control was appreciated. The essential principle (illustrated in Figure 2) is that the output of a power source, for instance a motor or a muscle, is controlled by a signal

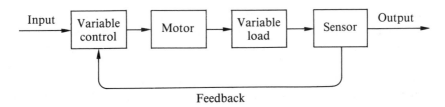

Feedback

Figure 2 A simple servo or feedback loop. The motor provides power, which is applied to a load that varies according to external conditions. The actual output is sensed and fed back to a variable control, which adjusts the power to meet variations in loading and thus maintains a constant output

derived from a discrepancy between the desired value of a variable and its current value. The humble thermostat which switches the boiler on when the temperature falls below the set point serves as a model for motor control in the peg-moving, bicycle riding, and many other tasks. In a purely feedback-controlled system the only information that needs to be stored in the CNS is the set point or goal since it is the environment which holds the information necessary to control movement.

Skills such as catching and hitting fast-moving objects and steering towards or around fixed objects provide some particularly clear examples of direct feedback control of movement. When moving through the environment, the visual field represented on the retina expands outwards from the centre, and similarly as an object approaches the observer textural features on its surface move from central towards peripheral vision. Lee and Young (1986) have shown in a variety of interception tasks that time to contact can be specified by the ratio of retinal size and expansion velocity of a textural feature, and that this variable (tau) is used to control movement directly.

The direct coupling of action to visual feedback is strikingly observed in tasks where mirrors, lenses, or closed-circuit television (CCTV) are used to change the familiar relationship between movement and the visual cues normally used to guide it. In tracing a star pattern seen in a mirror, subjects find it very difficult to change direction at the corners. One feels momentarily paralysed and further progress is possible only by decoupling the visual cue, that is, by not paying attention to it and allowing control to pass to the visual or kinaesthetic imagery system. Perceptual coupling is another way of relieving the motor system of its computational burden, and so we may conclude that both motor program theory and feedback theory have a range of possible answers to Bernstein's degrees of freedom problem.

Complex skills and control hierarchies

Feedback theory has been applied to a wider range of problems than just the control of simple motor acts. A complex skill, be it a straightforward sequence such as assembling a piece of equipment or a set of conditional actions such as might be employed in playing football or running a chemical plant, is characterized by a unique structure. Structured skills can be analysed into behavioural units called "TOTE" ("test-operate-test-exit") units by Miller, Galanter, and Pribram (1960) or "Operations" by Annett, Duncan, Stammers, and Gray (1971). Each unit is specified by a goal state of one or more variables, and the discrepancy between the goal state and the current state drives action. Consider the series of steps required to tie a bow, from grasping the two ends to be tied together to the final tug that tightens the knot (Annett, 1986). Each step can be thought of as a goal to be attained, having one end in each hand is necessary before proceeding to twist them together, and so on. Tying a bow is a simple behavioural sequence, but at the same time it has a vertical or hierarchical structure. A description of bow tying might refer to (1) making a half knot, (2) making two loops with the ends, and (3) making another half knot with the two loops. Stage (1) might be further broken down into sub-operations such as (1.1) grasping the free ends, (1.2) twisting one over the other, (1.3) pulling the half knot tight, and so on. It is even possible to break down (1.1) into detailed finger movements, although it would be less useful to specify these in detail because factors such as the size and flexibility of the material to be tied could vary, making it necessary to change some of the details from one knot to the next.

Serial organization and control

To assert that control of complex skills is hierarchically organized can give the misleading impression that all effective instructions issue from the highest level and are passed down to the effector units unchanged, but not even military hierarchies work in this way. Generals are responsible for strategy, not tactics, and units in a well-organized army have some degree of autonomy. Shaffer (1981) analysed the performance of highly skilled pianists by having them play a piano wired to a computer which timed each keystroke. They played pieces from memory and by sight and in different tempi and moods. A statistical analysis of the variations in the timing of keystrokes revealed that the temporal structure was most constant at the level of the bar, with much of the detailed variation in timing of particular bars being repeated across performances. Expressive temporal features, such as rubato, could be varied between performances while others were left unchanged. Shaffer interpreted these results as indicating that the temporal structure of the music is represented at an abstract level and is not simply determined by the speed with which one keystroke follows the next. In this sense the temporal features represent control at a relatively high level in the hierarchy.

THE ACQUISITION OF SKILLS

Skills are, by definition, learned, and in most cases must be specifically taught. The plasticity of skilled behaviour creates problems for theories of performance and is one of the main reasons for the abandonment of the 1950s-style linear information processing model. The pivotal concept of a capacity-limited information processing channel which could apparently account for choice reaction time data (Hick, 1952) and the trade-off between speed and accuracy in rapid movement tasks (Fitts, 1954) began to collapse when it was shown that extended practice changes the relationship between stimulus information and performance. Experimental results from thousands of trials of choice reaction time could no longer be fitted to Hick's equation

$$RT = k \log_2 (N + 1)$$

where k is a constant and N is the number of equiprobable stimuli requiring a unique response; it was also demonstrated that after weeks of practice two apparently conflicting tasks could be performed simultaneously.

Unfortunately, the investigation of learning was very closely identified with behaviourist concepts of stimulus, response, and reinforcement, and despite some early attempts to account for skill learning in information processing terms (Annett & Kay, 1957), it was not until the end of the 1960s that non-stimulus–response theories of skill acquisition began to emerge (Adams, 1971; Annett, 1969; Schmidt, 1975). These theories all referred to centrally stored data, the traces of previous sensory and motor events, and reinterpreted knowledge of results as information feedback which changes behaviour rather than reinforcement which acts by strengthening stimulus–response connections.

Mechanisms of learning

Practice results in both quantitative and qualitative changes in performance. Early studies with trainee morse telegraphists showed that the number of signals correctly transcribed per minute rises steadily over the first three to four months of practice, remains roughly constant (at a plateau) for the next two months, and then begins to rise again. The later acceleration in learning rate was accompanied by a change in method from transcribing single letters to receiving and writing down whole words. "Grouping", as this process came to be known, is one of the common qualitative changes in performance that results from practice.

A quantitative change occurs with practice in simple repetitive skills, so that the logarithm of time for each repetition is a linear function of the logarithm of the number of practice trials. This relationship is the *log-log-linear law of learning*, and its apparent simplicity suggests that there might be a single underlying learning process. Crossman (1959) suggested that each practice trial draws on a population of perceptual-motor processes and that these are evaluated in terms of the effort required to achieve the goal. On successive trials, each process is negatively weighted in proportion to the effort it entails, such that the probability of effortful processes being selected is progressively reduced. Newell and Rosenbloom (1981) maintained that a power function provides a better fit to skill acquisition data, including results from both motor and mental skills, and they propose that the learning principle is "chunking". Information is said to be chunked when it is dealt with as a single unit, for instance the telegraphist dealing in whole words rather than single letters. In terms of the hierarchical theory described earlier in the chapter, the lowest levels of the control hierarchy are chunked, thus a muscle synergy (a group of muscles operating together) would constitute a single chunk requiring only a single command rather than central specification of the activity in all the individual muscle units. It is hard to distinguish between the selection and the chunking theory on empirical grounds, but if one could look at changes in the detailed components of a skill as a function of practice, the Crossman theory would predict that more effortful components progressively give way to less effortful, whereas the Newell and Rosenbloom theory would predict that relatively stable and consistent groups of components would emerge after practice.

A single process would provide the most parsimonious account of learning, but there is ample evidence to suggest that there are at least two broadly different types of learning process, one type that occurs as a result of repetition *per se* and another in which cognition plays a major role. The log-log-linear law may well indicate not a single slow-acting process but a population of ways of learning that are successively drawn upon until exhausted. Thus, in the early stages, relatively rapid progress can be made by imitating the method of a skilled model or taking the advice of a coach, whereas much later in practice, when major sources of improvement have been exhausted, repetition may refine perceptual and temporal judgements or, according to a classical theory, facilitate the connections between task elements.

Cognitive processes

Observational learning and verbal instruction play an important part in the early stages of learning new skills (Fitts, 1964) but a well-articulated theory of cognitive motor learning is lacking, in part due to the lingering influence of behaviourism on theorizing about learning. Imitation occurs in a variety of animal and bird species, and in humans as young as 12 days (Meltzoff & Moore, 1977). The key to cognitive motor learning lies in elucidating the way in which learned skills are represented in memory.

Coaching hints can exploit the human capacity to form representations of objects and complex movement patterns. For example, a squash coach encourages his pupils to adopt a particular stance when receiving serve by instructing them to "pretend to be a Red Indian on the war-path". The phrase summons up an image of feet apart, knees slightly bent, right arm raised holding the racket/tomahawk head-high, and having a generally alert attitude. To the extent that learners (and you the reader) can both envisage the posture and adopt it is clear evidence of the existence of a high-level representation of a complex, but quite specific, movement pattern. These patterns, or "action prototypes" (Annett, 1979), are active in both the perception and production of actions, so if an action pattern is a perceptible entity it is (barring purely biomechanical limitations) capable of being produced. The theory that perception and action are served by the same rather than different processes has been entertained by a number of authors, for example Prinz (1986) and Weimer (1977). There is strong evidence that in perceiving the actions of other humans certain invariant features are extracted from the complex stimulus array. In a technique developed by Johansson (1973), an actor clad in dark clothes with small lights attached to the principal joints is filmed in high contrast. When the actor is stationary, only a jumble of bright spots is seen, but when the actor moves there is a distinct and immediate impression of human action. It has been shown (Cutting & Proffitt, 1982) that accurate judgements can be made about the actor's sex and the weight of any object being carried.

Studies of learning to ski (Whiting, Vogt, & Vereijken, 1992) illustrate how a learner can use an expert model as a source of information. The task was to learn a particular pattern of movement of the trunk and legs on a ski simulator. This device comprised a spring-loaded platform on which the learner stands and which slides from side to side over runners in response to leg and body movements. The movements were characterized by amplitude, frequency, and fluency the latter being a score derived from an idealized acceleration pattern. All subjects were given knowledge of results on the three scores (frequency, amplitude, and fluency) and all improved with practice, but the subjects who observed the model quickly learned to match the fluency characteristic, although even after five practice sessions, few subjects were able to match the precise frequency and amplitude of the model's movements. This ability to abstract a particular higher-order description or representation of a complex activity is crucial to imitation, but more experimental studies are needed, particularly studies that relate subjects' ability to perceive significant features of action to the ability to perform that action.

Verbal instruction

Motor *skill* is conventionally distinguished from verbal *knowledge* and the former is often inaccessible to the latter. Skilled swimmers cannot answer factual questions about the breast-stroke any faster or more accurately than novices, and subjects can learn to control complex systems, including simulated chemical plant and transportation systems, without being able to express the rules that govern their control decisions.

Neurological evidence points to the likelihood of separate encoding of verbal knowledge and motor capability in the central nervous system. Amnesics who cannot recall facts can learn and remember a motor skill (Cohen & Squire, 1980), and one consequence of damage to the corpus callosum which connects the two hemispheres of the brain is that patients have difficulty in following verbal instructions to carry out simple tasks with the left hand (which is controlled by the right, non-verbal, hemisphere). The problem of how the verbal and non-verbal systems communicate is a matter of conjecture, but it seems likely that the translation is effected through the mechanisms of high-level representations that include both images and abstractions. Experts asked (for the first time at least) to explain how a task is performed frequently resort to imagery, whereas instructors, as was shown in the "Red Indian" example above, often resort to imagery-inducing language in order to convey information about postures and actions.

Knowledge of results

Perhaps the most extensive use of language in skill training is in the provision of knowledge of results, and this topic has received very extensive coverage in the research literature (see summaries by Annett, 1969; Salmoni, Schmidt, & Walter, 1984). Informing the learner of the outcome of each response or trial (knowledge of results, or KR) typically gives the most rapid learning, whereas no-KR, or practice-only conditions, generally show poor learning or none at all. The rate and extent of learning is sensitive to the amount of information given – the more detailed the KR the better the learning – making it clear that the "reinforcement" interpretation is inadequate.

Several theories stress the informative properties of KR. Annett (1969) interpreted KR as a form of feedback used by the learner to adapt responses to the standard specified by the trainer. This very simple theory applied to the acquisition of a linear positioning task proposes a short-term store of the kinaesthetic sensations produced by the preceding movement and the simple strategy of modifying the direction and approximate extent of the next movement according to a simple rule that uses both external KR and internal feedback. The first attempt to produce a movement of the specified extent is guided only by a pre-existing concept of the required direction and amplitude but the second attempt is based on (1) a (fading) memory trace of the first attempt, (2) discrimination between internal feedback from a current response and the trace of the preceding response, and (3) a simple strategy such as, "if the last response was shorter than required make the next one longer, if it was correct reproduce it, if it was too long make it shorter". Evidence from the rate and extent of learning linear positioning tasks with different kinds and amounts of KR provides qualitative support for this basic model.

Adams's (1971) theory, also based on the concept of feedback, proposes a "motor trace" or record of the output specification of a response and a "perceptual trace", a record of the sensory feedback (including KR) associated with that motor trace. Practice strengthens the perceptual trace such that the sensory consequences of motor outputs are anticipated. Outputs can then be preselected on the basis of their expected feedback. Schmidt's "schema theory" (Schmidt, 1975) extended Adams's "closed loop theory" to account for the learning of classes of actions. The choice of motor output is related to expected sensory consequences by information about previous response specifications, previous sensory consequences, and previous outcomes, that is, whether the sensory consequences signal a desired state of affairs. These sources of information are consolidated into a "recognition schema" that encodes the relationships between sensory consequences and outcomes, and a recall schema that relates outcomes to response specifications. The particular merit of the schema theory is that it allows for generalized learning and it makes the specific prediction that learning is most effective when a variety of responses are made, thus practising throwing darts at different targets is as good or better than just practising with the bullseye. This prediction is by and large fulfilled, but none of the three theories makes very strong differential predictions; it can be argued that they provide only a general description of the learning mechanism.

A later theoretical development was the application of connectionist models to simple motor learning. Horak (1992) used a simulated neural network to represent Schmidt's recall schema in learning a unidimensional ballistic skill such as throwing an object at a target at some (variable) distance. The network learns to match its variable force output to different inputs, representing different target distances, by changing the weights of interconnections between its elements (analogous to individual neurons) according to performance outcomes. In a sense, the network discovers the rule relating perceived target distance to appropriate force output in much the same way as suggested by Annett's (1969) account of the role of KR in learning. An especially intriguing feature of this simulation is that it exhibits the *contextual interference effect*. That is, if trials involving roughly the same distance and requiring similar force are given in a block, the network learns quite rapidly but transfers less well to targets set at other distances than when trials at different distances are varied randomly in the practice sequence. In the latter case, learning rate is reduced but transfer between targets at different distances is improved and in this respect the network model mimics the qualitative results of actual learning experiments.

Much of the research on KR has used simple unidimensional positioning tasks, but in more complex skills, such as gymnastics, outcome information may be insufficient to identify critical features of the performance that need to be modified. Kinematic data may be helpful but, as with video recordings, may need expert interpretation to establish the precise link between performance and outcome.

KR is often said to have a motivational role. Even when not very informative, KR seems to boost performance by encouraging persistence in effortful and monotonous tasks (see Annett, 1969, chap. 5). If KR provides information about goal attainment, there is no need to postulate an additional energizing function to account for learning. In the context of current theories of skill as goal-directed action it is unlikely that any activity that is not seen to be making progress towards some goal will be maintained, especially if it consumes resources of energy or information processing capacity, thus in any comparison between KR and no-KR conditions performance under the latter is likely to be less effortful, less concentrated and less persistent. The motivational effect of KR is simply a demonstration of "feedback in action" (Annett, 1969).

RETENTION AND TRANSFER

Motor memory

It is a common observation that a skill once learned is never forgotten. Early studies of typewriting and juggling, using the relearning or *savings* method, showed that after more than a year without practice the level of performance originally reached after 45–50 days of practice was regained with about 10 days of retraining, a saving of 80 per cent of the original learning. Hill (1957), using himself as a subject, measured savings of 70 per cent in typing skill over a retention interval of 50 years! Retention of verbal material is typically less good. A study by Leavitt and Schlosberg (1944) apparently confirmed the superiority of motor memory by comparing savings scores for pursuit rotor tracking and nonsense syllable learning after intervals of 1, 7, 28, and 70 days. They found that retention of the motor task declined from near 90 per cent after a retention interval of 1 day to around 75 per cent after 70 days, whereas savings on the nonsense syllables declined from about 80 per cent after 1 day to 50 per cent after 70 days. This result is not, however, as clear-cut as it at first appears since the two tasks were not equated for ease of learning nor for the number of trials or repetitions, and both these factors are known to affect retention.

Short-term retention of skills (short-term motor memory – STMM) has been studied largely through the medium of simple positioning tasks in which subjects attempt to reproduce movements of a specific extent, normally without the aid of vision. Variables such as number of repetitions, duration of the retention interval, and interference have yielded a body of information on kinaesthetic memory and the central, but not very conclusive, debate has been how movement information is encoded, for example as action plans

70

(motor programs) or sensory templates. The evidence (e.g., Laabs, 1973) suggests that what is retained is the location of a target rather than the extent of the movement required to reach it, that is, a spatial rather than strictly motor or kinaesthetic memory.

Using a task analogous to digit span (which entails memorizing short strings of digits), Smyth and Pendleton (1990) found evidence to suggest that memory for bodily movements, such as dance steps, may be distinct from memory for spatial location. Subjects observed, and were asked after a short interval to reproduce, a series of arbitrary body movements. Various interference tasks during the short retention interval reduced the number of items correctly recalled but in different degrees. Verbal interference tasks had little effect, whereas motor tasks such as squeezing a rubber bulb, pointing to a series of targets and watching, or making similar movements, reduced the number of items correctly recalled. The results of the experiments as a whole suggest a dissociation between verbal, spatial and movement coding systems in short-term memory.

Although absolute values of felt force, distance, and direction can be retained with moderate accuracy for short periods, it is unlikely that we rely on simple sensori-motor memory of discrete movements to remember how to perform skilled tasks. The world in which we live and the actions we need to take are far too variable for it to be worthwhile to memorize precise movement information. It is rather through a set of outline plans organized so as to achieve criterion conditions, which may be abstractly defined, that we are able to remember how to solve familiar motor problems (Annett, 1988).

Transfer of training

The element of non-specificity in skill learning makes it possible to transfer the benefits of experience in one situation to others that are related. Having learned to drive a Mini, only a little more training is needed to master a Jaguar or a Rolls Royce; indeed, our whole system of education and training is based on the presumption of transfer, that is, that acquiring some specific skills will enhance the acquisition of others. Transfer of training, like retention, can be measured in terms of the savings in learning Task B that can be attributed to prior experience on Task A. According to Woodworth (1938), E. H. Weber, the father of psychophysics, reported in the 1840s that skills learned with the right hand transferred to the left and vice versa, and that a surgeon trained his students to carry out difficult operations with the left hand so that they would be better able to perform them with the right (see Woodworth & Schlosberg, 1955, pp. 738–743).

The traditional theory of transfer was that practice on any task will develop one or more abilities and that the transfer task will benefit to the extent that it also depends on the same ability. This *formal discipline theory* was at the basis of educational practice, popular at least since the time of

John Locke, which insisted on learning poetry to develop the memory and mathematics to develop logical thinking. An alternative theory of *identical elements* is that transfer occurs only when the original learning task and the transfer task share some common feature or element. Under the influence of behaviourism, the elements soon came to be understood as stimuli and responses and from this narrow interpretation arose the paradox of *negative transfer*.

Negative transfer occurs when previous experience interferes with the learning or performance of a skill, and this can happen when transferring between tasks that are similar in all but a few important respects, such as transferring from a right-hand-drive car to a left-hand-drive, or even changing from driving on the left to driving on the right side of the road. In such cases almost every element is identical. However, a problem can arise when near-identical stimuli must be linked to different responses, for example moving a lever in the opposite direction to that originally learned. For transfer to occur, not only is it important that the two tasks should have common stimuli and responses, but also they should have common stimulus–response connections.

Even with this modification, the identical elements theory is not entirely satisfactory because of the occasional failure of transfer even when the tasks concerned have important common elements (Annett & Sparrow, 1985). Fotheringhame (1984), for example, found no significant transfer between two measurement tasks employing the same principles (the use of micrometers and vernier height gauges) unless the principle linking the two was explicitly taught. The additional, and perhaps essential, factor in transfer is an *awareness* of features or elements common to the old and the new task, and here the trainer or educator can employ training techniques likely to enhance useful transfer (Annett & Sparrow, 1985).

It has been suggested that learning often occurs at two levels, a cognitive and a *meta*cognitive level. Metacognition refers to awareness of one's own cognitive processes, thus it is possible both to learn a skill and to know something about how one is doing it and to have a learning strategy. Less able learners and those who show poor generalization and transfer typically have underdeveloped metacognitive skills (Downs & Perry, 1985), and training programmes in metacognitive skills are being developed for use in schools and the training of less able school-leavers. The role that metacognition might play in the acquisition and transfer of perceptual-motor skills is, however, relatively unexplored territory.

CONCLUSION

Any introductory review of such a broad and active field as motor skill is bound to be incomplete. Little has been said in this survey about the problems that technological advances bring to modern industrial skills or

72

about issues in education and rehabilitation. In the early 1950s researchers in motor skills were among the first to see the relevance of information processing concepts to our understanding of human motor performance. In doing so they provided an important building block for modern cognitive psychology, but it was only later that relations between cognition and skill were explored in depth. The Cartesian dichotomy of body and mind would relegate motor skill to mere mechanism, not involving truly psychological processes, but a conception of skill is emerging that interprets the mechanisms of movement in the context of meaningful action. This recognition of the importance of cognitive processes in the generation and control of action and in the acquisition of skill is leading to exciting new research prospects.

FURTHER READING

Holding, D. H. (1989). *Human skills* (2nd edn). Chichester: Wiley.
Jeannerod, M. (1988). *The neural and behavioural organisation of goal-directed movements*. Oxford: Oxford University Press.
Jeannerod, M. (1990). *Attention and performance: XIII. Motor representation and control*. Hillside, NJ: Lawrence Erlbaum.
Rosenbaum, D. (1991). *Human motor control*. London: Academic Press.
Summers, J. J. (1992). *Approaches to the study of motor control and learning*. Amsterdam: Elsevier.

REFERENCES

Abernethy, B., & Sparrow, W. A. (1992). The rise and fall of dominant paradigms in motor behaviour research. In J. J. Summers (Ed.) *Approaches to the study of motor control and learning* (pp. 3–45). Amsterdam: Elsevier.
Adams, J. A. (1971). A closed loop theory of motor learning. *Journal of Motor Behavior, 3,* 111–150.
Annett, J. (1969). *Feedback and human behaviour*. Harmondsworth: Penguin.
Annett, J. (1979). Memory for skill. In M. M. Gruneberg & P. E. Morris (Eds) *Applied problems in memory* (pp. 215–247). London: Academic Press.
Annett, J. (1986). On knowing how to do things. In H. Heuer & C. Fromm (Eds) *Generation and modulation of action patterns* (pp. 187–200). Berlin: Springer.
Annett, J. (1988). Motor learning and retention. In M. M. Gruneberg, P. E. Morris, & R. N. Sykes (Eds) *Practical aspects of memory: Current research and issues. Clinical and educational implications* (vol. 2, pp. 434–440). Chichester: Wiley.
Annett, J., & Kay, H. (1957). Knowledge of results and skilled performance. *Occupational Psychology, 31,* 69–79.
Annett, J., & Sparrow, J. (1985). Transfer of training: A review of research and practical implications. *Programmed Learning and Educational Technology, 22,* 116–124.
Annett, J., Duncan, K. D., Stammers, R. B., & Gray, M. J. (1971). *Task analysis*. Department of Employment training information paper 6. London: Her Majesty's Stationery Office.
Bell, C. (1826). On the nervous circle which connects the voluntary muscles with the brain. *Philosophic Transactions, 2,* 163–173.

Bernstein, N. (1967). *The coordination and regulation of movements.* Oxford: Pergamon.

Bizzi, E. (1980). Central and peripheral mechanisms in motor control. In G. E. Stelmach & J. Requin (Eds) *Tutorials in motor behavior* (pp. 131–143). Amsterdam: North Holland.

Brooks, V. B. (1986). *The neural basis of motor control.* Oxford: Oxford University Press.

Cohen, N. J., & Squire, L. R. (1980). Preserved learning and retention of pattern analyzing skill in amnesia: Dissociation of knowing how and knowing that. *Science, 210*, 207–210.

Corkin, S. (1968). Acquisition of motor skills after bilateral medial temporal lobe excision. *Neurospychologia, 6*, 255–265.

Craik, K. J. W. (1947). Theory of the human operator in control systems: 1. The operator as an engineering system. *British Journal of Psychology, 38*, 56–61.

Crossman, E. R. F. W. (1959). A theory of the acquisition of speed skill. *Ergonomics, 2*, 153–166.

Cutting, J. E., & Proffitt, D. R. (1982). The minimum principle and the perception of absolute, common and relative motion. *Cognitive Psychology, 14*, 211–286.

Downs, S., & Perry, P. (1985). *Developing skilled learners: Learning to learn in the YTS.* Sheffield: Manpower Services Commission R&D no. 22.

Fitts, P. M. (1954). The information capacity of the human motor system in controlling the amplitude of movement. *Journal of Experimental Psychology, 47*, 381–391.

Fitts, P. M. (1964). Perceptual motor skill learning. In A. W. Melton (Ed.) *Categories of human learning* (pp. 234–285). New York: Academic Press.

Fotheringhame, J. (1984). Transfer of training: A field investigation. *Occupational Psychology, 57*, 239–248.

Hick, W. E. (1952). On the rate of gain of information. *Quarterly Journal of Experimental Psychology, 4*, 11–26.

Hill, L. B. (1957). A second quarter century of delayed recall or relearning at eighty. *Journal of Educational Psychology, 48*, 65–68.

Horak, M. (1992). The utility of connectionism for motor learning: A reinterpretation of contextual interference in movement schemes. *Journal of Motor Behavior, 24*(1), 58–66.

Johansson, G. (1973). Visual perception of biological motion and a model for its analysis. *Perception and Psychophysics, 14*, 201–211.

Laabs, G. J. (1973). Retention characteristics of different reproduction cues in motor short-term memory. *Journal of Experimental Psychology, 100*, 168–177.

Lashley, K. S. (1917). The accuracy of movement in the absence of excitation from the moving organ. *American Journal of Physiology, 43*, 169–194.

Laszlo, J. I. (1966). The performance of simple motor task with kinaesthetic sense loss. *Quarterly Journal of Experimental Psychology, 18*, 1–8.

Leavitt, H. J., & Schlosberg, H. (1944). The retention of verbal and motor skills. *Journal of Experimental Psychology, 34*, 404–417.

Lee, D. N., & Young, D. S. (1986). Gearing action to the environment. In H. Heuer & C. Fromm (Eds) *Generation and modulation of action patterns* (pp. 217–230). Berlin: Springer.

Lee, D. N., Lishman, J. R., & Thomson, J. A. (1982). Regulation of gait in long jumping. *Journal of Experimental Psychology: Human Perception and Performance, 8*, 448–459.

Meltzoff, A. N., & Moore, M. K. (1977). Imitation of facial and manual gestures. *Science, 198*, 75–80.

Miller, G. A., Galanter, E., & Pribram, K. (1960). *Plans and the structure of behavior*. New York: Holt, Reinhart & Winston.

Newell, A., & Rosenbloom, P. S. (1981). Mechanisms of skill acquisition and the law of practice. In J. R. Anderson (Ed.) *Cognitive skills and their acquisition* (pp. 1–55). Hillsdale, NJ: Lawrence Erlbaum.

Paillard, J. (1982). Apraxia and the neurophysiology of motor control. *Philosophical Transactions of the Royal Society of London*, B298, 111–134.

Paillard, J. (Ed.) (1991). *Brain and space*. Oxford: Oxford University Press.

Prinz, W. (1986). Modes of linkage between perception and action. In W. Prinz, & A. F. Sanders (Eds) *Cognition and motor processes* (pp. 185–193). Berlin: Springer.

Salmoni, A. W., Schmidt, R. A., & Walter, C. B. (1984). Knowledge of results and motor learning: A review and critical appraisal. *Psychological Bulletin*, *95*, 355–386.

Schmidt, R. A. (1975). A schema theory of discrete motor skill learning. *Psychological Review*, *82*, 225–260.

Shaffer, L. H. (1981). Performances of Chopin, Bach, and Bartok: Studies in motor programming. *Cognitive Psychology*, *13*, 326–376.

Smyth, M. M., & Pendleton, L. R. (1990). Space and movement in working memory. *Quarterly Journal of Experimental Psychology*, *42A*, 291–304.

Summers, J. J. (1989). Motor programs. In D. H. Holding (Ed.) *Human skills* (2nd edn, pp. 49–59). Chichester: Wiley.

Vredenbregt, J., & Koster, W. G. (1971). Analysis and synthesis of handwriting. *Philips Technical Review*, *32*, 73–78.

Wadman, W. J., Denier, C., van der Gon, J. J., Geuze, R. H., & Moll, C. R. (1979). Control of fast goal-directed arm movements. *Journal of Human Movement Studies*, *5*, 3–17.

Weimer, W. B. (1977). A conceptual framework for cognitive psychology: motor theories of the mind. In R. Shaw & J. Bransford (Eds) *Perceiving, acting and knowing: Towards an ecological psychology* (pp. 267–311). Hillsdale, NJ: Lawrence Erlbaum.

Whiting, H. T. A., Vogt, S., & Vereijken, B. (1992). Human skill and motor control: Some aspects of the motor control–motor learning relation. In J. J. Summers (Ed.) *Approaches to the study of motor control and learning* (pp. 81–111). Amsterdam: Elsevier.

Woodworth, R. S. (1938). *Experimental psychology*. London: Methuen.

Woodworth. R. S., & Schlosberg, H. (1955). *Experimental psychology* (3rd edn). London: Methuen.

5

SOCIAL SKILLS

Michael Argyle
University of Oxford, England

Social skills are patterns of social behaviour which make individuals socially competent, that is, able to produce the desired effects on other people. These effects may be related to personal motivations, for example, to be popular, or to task goals, for example, to enhance learning, recovery, or hard work on the part of others. Everyday social skills are mainly about the first, professional skills about the second.

It has been known for some time that social skills can have powerful effects on personal life, including mental health, as well as on successful work performance. As a result there has been a rapid increase in the use of social skills training, for many kinds of patients, for many types of work, and also for loneliness, for heterosexual skills, and for working abroad. We shall discuss later the methods used, and how far they are successful.

"Social skills" is also a model of social behaviour, which uses the analogy between social performance and motor skills, like driving a car (Argyle, 1983). This and other models of social performance will be discussed later. Social skills are usually regarded as the behavioural side of social competence; there are other components, such as knowledge and understanding and the absence of anxiety, which contribute to competence, and lie behind skilled performance.

THE ASSESSMENT OF SOCIAL COMPETENCE

It is necessary to assess individuals' social competence, in order to decide if and how they should be trained, and in order to do research into social skills. The methods which are commonly used are different for the study and training of people at work, and for clinical settings, including loneliness and other everyday problems.

Social skills at work

These may be assessed by research workers, for example studying the effects of different kinds of supervision, or for personnel selection and promotion. *Objective measures of effectiveness*, such as sales, productivity, or other performance measures, have the advantage of face validity – of being direct indices of success on the job. However, it may be difficult to obtain such measures: different individuals may be working in different situations so that the measures are not comparable, and it may be necessary to consider a range of outcomes, some of them difficult to measure, like "goodwill" (for sales). Nevertheless in many work situations it is objective results which often lead to promotion or redundancy.

Ratings by subordinates or colleagues are used in merit rating incentive schemes, and have often been used in leadership research, such as the Fleishman and Harris (1962) Leader Behavior Description Questionnaire.

77

Such ratings can include a wide range of scales, but it needs to be known which if any are relevant aspects of social skills.

Role-playing is often used in management selection, in assessment centres, with role-playing as leaders or members of work-groups or committees, or dealing with analogue work situations. It has been found to be a good predictor of management success, correlating with management success in the range .25–.35 (Muchinsky, 1986), and also correlates well with behaviour on the job, such as for teachers.

Video role-play can be used when it is difficult to create scaled-down versions of some jobs for role-play purposes; in this there is a video-presentation of a problem, to which the candidate makes spoken replies that are recorded and rated. This has been done in Britain for the police (Bull & Horncastle, 1983).

Interviews are widely used to assess work skills: it is probably a mistake to base judgements on performance in the interview, since it is an unusual situation. It is better to ask for detailed accounts of performance in situations at work or in other similar situations.

SOCIAL SKILLS FOR PATIENTS AND THE GENERAL POPULATION

Interviews can be a rich source of information, to find out the situations or relationships which are found difficult, and what seems to go wrong. *Role-playing* is also often used, with local "stooges" or other trainees, either modelling the situations found difficult, or an open-ended "get to know the other" task. This is video-taped and studied carefully. It is now known that role-played behaviour has only a modest relationship for patients with performance in natural settings (McNamara & Blumer, 1982); nevertheless trainers find it a rich source of data. A more elaborate alternative is the Social Interaction Test, in which patients are confronted by standard social situations (Trower, Bryant, & Argyle, 1978).

A large number of self-report *questionnaires* have been constructed, mostly in the USA, for social competence, usually with between three and seven subscales. These are reviewed by Spitzberg and Cupach (1989). At the present time little is known about their validity and no scales have become generally accepted, or come into clinical use. A short and simple scale, which has had some success as a research measure is the Social Competence Questionnaire (Sarason, Sarason, Hacker, & Basham 1985). Argyle, Furnham, and Graham (1981) used a self-report measure of degrees of difficulty experienced in different social situations – information which is needed by a trainer (Table 1). There is a little more agreement on measures of the main components of social skills, like empathy and assertiveness, and these will be described later.

Table 1 List of difficult situations

1	Complaining to a neighbour who you know well about constant noisy disturbances
2	Taking a person of the opposite sex out for the first time for an evening
3	Going for a job interview
4	Visiting the doctor when unwell
5	Going to close relative's funeral
6	Going round to cheer up a depressed friend who asked you to call
7	Being a host or hostess at a large party (e.g., twenty-first birthday)
8	Give a short formal speech to a group of about fifty people that you don't know
9	Taking an unsatisfactory article back to a shop where you purchased it
10	Going across to introduce yourself to new neighbours
11	Dealing with a difficult and disobedient child
12	Going to a function with many people from a different culture
13	Playing a party game after dinner (charades, musical chairs)
14	Attending a distant relation's wedding ceremony when you know few people
15	Apologizing to a superior for forgetting an important errand

Source: Argyle, Furnham, and Graham, 1981

Finally *ratings by others* can sometimes be made: for example, teachers can rate pupils, pupils can rate each other, and hospital staff can rate patients.

THE NEED FOR TRAINING IN SOCIAL SKILLS

How many people need training – assuming that this can be done successfully? In one sense everyone's skills could be improved, just as opera singers have teachers and Olympic athletes have coaches. However, there is a smaller group whose lack of social skills is more acute, and who suffer as a result.

In the general population

1 *Children* – who are rejected, usually because they are aggressive or disruptive, or who are isolated, or who have no close friends.
2 *Adolescents and young people* – who are lonely, shy, unassertive, or have heterosexual problems. About 40 per cent of students say they are "shy", 55 per cent are often lonely (Argyle, 1984). This is one of the largest groups with social skills problems.
3 *Adults* – who have no friends, or marital difficulties (one-third of couples break up), or can't cope with their children.
4 *Old people* – who are lonely, have difficulty keeping up relations with kin, or are quarrelsome.

Failures in some of these spheres produce great unhappiness and have further consequences: marriages break up, badly handled children become delinquent, and isolated children and young people become mentally disturbed.

Social skills at work

Most jobs involve dealing with people; for teachers, managers, salespeople, and others this is the main task. Socially unskilled managers produce high levels of discontent, and consequent absenteeism and labour turnover among their subordinates. Some salespeople sell four times as much as others, in the same shop. Those who go to work abroad, as salespeople or for organizations like the Peace Corps, have a failure rate of 60 per cent or more in some parts of the Far East and Middle East, that is, they come home before their one- or two-year term is completed (Argyle, 1984). Lack of social skills is one of the main reasons that people lose their jobs. Many jobs require special skills: the only alternative to training is trying to learn these skills on the job by trial and error; evidently this often fails.

Mental patients

All kinds of mental patients have social behaviour problems. Schizophrenics are the worst, and are found very difficult to interact with. Depressives are also found very unrewarding. Many neurotics have social skills deficits. Bryant, Trower, Yardley, Urbieta, and Letemendia (1976) found that 17 per cent of adult neurotics (on a conservative estimate) were socially inadequate in a number of ways, corresponding to the components of social skill (described below) such as low rewardingness or assertiveness, inadequate non-verbal communication, and poor conversational powers.

THE COMPONENTS OF SOCIAL SKILL

What are the basic psychological processes which generate socially skilled behaviour? If we knew the answer, it would be easier to measure and train social skills. There is no agreed answer to this question, though each of the processes described below has been put forward by a number of people, sometimes under different names.

The social skill model

This model uses motor skills, like riding a bicycle or driving a car, as a model for social skills (Figure 1). In each case the performer seeks certain goals (e.g., make others talk a lot), makes skilled moves (e.g., asks closed questions), perceives the effects of this (e.g., short replies), and takes corrective action (e.g., asks more open-ended questions). The model emphasizes the goals of interactors, the specific social behaviour used, and the perception of

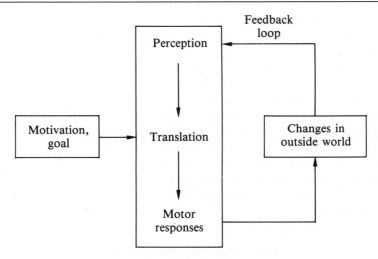

Figure 1 Motor skill model
Source: Argyle, 1983

and reactions to feedback. In the example above the questioner modified the kind of questions asked, just as a driver might adjust the steering wheel of a car. There is continuous flexibility of behaviour in response to the behaviour of the other (Argyle, 1983).

This model has led to emphasis on the elements of social performance, particularly the non-verbal ones, like facial expression and gaze. However, it has become clear that verbal elements are also important, and that global aspects of performance, such as rewardingness and assertiveness, may be more important than any specific elements. We also know that a number of further processes need to be taken into account. Some of these are about particular goals (e.g., assertiveness), others about particular behaviours (e.g., non-verbal communication), or about other parts of the model (e.g., cognition).

Assertiveness

Assertiveness, the ability to influence or control others, has sometimes been equated with social competence. It is contrasted both with aggression and with passive behaviour; a number of scales have been devised which have some validity against behaviour (e.g., Rathus, 1973). It was first introduced by behaviour therapists, in the belief that assertiveness inhibits anxiety, it has been taken up by women to overcome alleged oppression by men (men do score higher on assertiveness scales), and it has been found useful for some professional training, such as for nurses (Galassi, Galassi, & Vedder, 1981).

Lazarus (1973) proposed that assertiveness has four main components: refusing requests, asking for favours and making requests, expressing positive and negative feelings, and initiating, continuing, and ending general conversation. Assertiveness is found to correlate with a range of non-verbal elements (e.g. louder voice, more gaze), and with verbal ones. However, I shall draw instead on the social psychology of social influence. At the heart of any form of social influence there must be a verbal request; to be effective this needs to be persuasive, that is, it motivates and persuades by offering some good reason or incentive for complying with the request. The verbal request should be accompanied by the appropriate non-verbal style, such as tone of voice – a combination of dominant and friendly. Influence is greater if there is already a strong interpersonal relationship of friendship, authority, or both, though this may be strengthened in "ingratiation", where the request is preceded by flattery and agreement. The request should be an appropriate and legitimate one.

Rewardingness, reinforcement

Social psychologists have often regarded this as the key to friendship and interpersonal attraction. Jennings (1950), in a classic study of 400 girls in a reformatory, found that the popular girls were the ones who helped, protected, cheered, and encouraged others. Several theories of interpersonal attraction are based on findings like this. Leadership skills include a dimension of "Consideration", that is, looking after the needs of group members. Marital therapy has often consisted of training spouses in providing greater rewards for one another. Mental patients, especially schizophrenics and depressives, are found to be very unrewarding and "socially bankrupt".

The effect of reinforcement in social situations is to keep others in the situation or relationship, to increase the other's attraction to ego, and to make greater influence possible, when reinforcement is contingent on the desired behaviour. It can take a variety of forms. Verbal reinforcement includes praise, approval, acceptance, agreement, encouragement, and sympathy. Non-verbal rewards are smiles, head-nods, gaze, touch (in some situations), and tone of voice. Rewards can also take the form of help, presents, meals, advice, and information. Engaging in enjoyable shared activities is also rewarding, for example, sport, dancing, music and parties (Hargie, Saunders, & Dickson, 1987).

Non-verbal communication (NVC)

The social moves or signals of the social skills model are partly non-verbal, and perception and feedback is partly of the NVC of others. Assertiveness and rewardingness require special non-verbal styles of voice, face and posture. There is found to be a general factor of non-verbal expressiveness consisting of

1 a lot of facial expression, especially smiling
2 a high level of gaze
3 closer proximity
4 voice louder, higher pitch, more expressive
5 more other-directed gestures, fewer self-directed (e.g., self-touching).

Socially competent and effective people of all kinds are higher on this factor: doctors, teachers, and others do better if they have it. Socially inadequate people are low on it (Argyle, 1988). There is a self-report scale of expressiveness by Friedman, Prince, Riggio, & DiMatteo (1980); people in jobs needing social skills have a higher score. However, it is necessary for such people to be able to control their non-verbal expression: air stewardesses do this partly by simply adopting the appropriate expression, partly by thinking positive thoughts about the passengers (Hochschild, 1983).

It is necessary to decode the NVC of others correctly. There is some evidence that this is important, and some patients are very bad at it, but it is less important than effective encoding. There are several tests of such perceptual sensitivity, such as the PONS test (Rosenthal, Hall, DiMatteo, Rogers, and Archer, 1979), but there is little correlation between these different measures.

Another kind of NVC is used in conjunction with speech, and is described below; non-verbal signals are also used as the main vehicle for self-presentation.

Verbal communication

This lies at the heart of nearly all human social performance and social skill. Most skilled moves or signals are basically verbal, and furthermore have to fit into a conversational sequence. Even one utterance has to be skilfully designed, to be understandable by the recipient. It is a "speech act", a piece of behaviour planned to have some effect on the others. Encoding requires anticipatory decoding. Professional skills, like those of teachers, psychotherapists, or trade union negotiators, need special verbal skills. Socially inadequate individuals are often very poor conversationalists. However, no measure has so far been produced for verbal skills.

Effective management of conversational sequences is important. There are certain common two-step sequences like question–answer. Grice (1975) put forward rules for acceptable utterances: they should be relevant to what went before, provide enough information but not too much, be clear, and true. The social skills model suggests a basic four-step sequence, where the first speaker corrects his first move at step 3.

1 Interviewer: asks question
2 Respondent: gives inadequate answer, or fails to understand

83

3 Interviewer: clarifies and repeats question
4 Respondent: gives more adequate answer.

Another important type of skilled move is the "proactive" or double speech act, for example, where a speaker replies to a question and then asks one in return, instead of bringing the conversation to a halt. Some professional social skills, like teaching, involve repeated cycles, such as repetition of the following: teacher lectures – teacher asks question (a proactive move) – pupil replies (Flanders, 1970).

It is normal for speakers to "accommodate" to each other's speech style, to speak at a more similar speed, loudness, accent, language, and so on. This happens when people like each other or want to be accepted, and it does lead to greater acceptance (Giles & Coupland, 1991).

One of the main ways in which Grice's rules are broken is in the interest of "politeness". The main purpose of politeness is avoiding damaging the other's self-esteem, and it is done by avoiding constraining his or her behaviour, for example by indirect requests ("mitigation"), by praising the other rather than self, and by maximizing agreement. Such politeness is effective, for example in preserving relations between captain and crew of aircraft, though in times of crisis, mitigation should be replaced by "aggravation": "Turn the bloody engine off", not "Excuse me, captain, but how about turning the engine off?" (Linde, 1988).

Conversation is closely coordinated with, and supported by, non-verbal signals. Speakers accompany their words with illustrative gestures, vocal emphasis, and intonation; they look up at grammatical breaks, and at the ends of utterances, to obtain back-channel feedback. Listeners provide continuous feedback by facial expressions, occasional vocalizations, head-nods, and posture. Turn-taking is managed by speakers giving terminal gazes at the ends of utterances, falling pitch, and return of hands to rest, as well as by the verbal structure of utterances (Argyle, 1988).

Empathy, cooperation, and concern for others

Empathy is the capacity to share the perceived emotion of another, and to understand the point of view of others, to "take the role of the other" (Eisenberg & Strayer, 1987). There are a number of measures, of which the best known is that devised by Mehrabian and Epstein (1972). Undue attention to self, including an inability to take much interest in others or their point of view, is found in all kinds of mental patients. In psychotherapy, interviewing, and many other skills, it is important to pay careful attention to the views and feelings of others, and to display this by questions, "reflection", and other techniques.

Cooperation is taking account of the goals of others, as well as one's own, and coordinating behaviour so that both shall be reached. All social activities take more than one to do them, whether play (e.g., see-saw, tennis), social activity (dancing, singing, talking, sex), or work of most kinds. Many kinds of social skill failure can be seen as failure of cooperation. Social life calls for a lot of cooperation:

> You're on a bike hike with five of your friends. One of the girls, who just moved into the neighbourhood, is very slow and is holding the group up. The other girls you are with are all yelling at her and threatening to leave her behind. (Dodge, no date)

One solution might be simply to slow down with her.

Successful leadership skills involve consulting and persuading subordinates. Negotiation consists of finding an "integrative" solution, where each side makes concessions, so that the main goals of each are attained (Argyle, 1991). Concern for others is central to all close relationships; much social skills training (SST) for patients and lonely people is basically about establishing such relationships. In love, marriage, and close friendships, conceptualized as "communal" relationships, social influence and exchange of rewards are less important than concern for the needs of the other (Hays, 1988).

Cognition and problem solving

Cognitive social psychology has become important for the study of judgements and attitudes. How important is it for social skills? A number of aspects of social skill lie outside the field of consciousness, and are evidently the result of lower-level processes. People cannot tell us how they manage to take turns, follow the rules of grammar, respond to small non-verbal signals, fall in love, or manage other relationships (Argyle, 1988; Nisbett & Wilson, 1977), any more than they can explain how they walk or ride a bicycle. In both cases the lower levels are automatic, the higher ones governed by plans and rules.

There are areas of social skill where cognitive factors have been found to be important. First, there are informal rules of behaviour, of which people are aware; if the rules of relationships are broken, the relationship is likely to be disrupted. In the case of friendship, Argyle, Henderson, and Furnham (1985) found that "third party rules" are particularly important – keep confidences, don't criticize others in public, don't be jealous of other relationships, and so on. Second, it is important to understand the true nature of situations and relationships. La Gaipa and Wood (1981) found that disturbed adolescents, who had no friends, had inadequate ideas about friendship: like younger children they thought it was about receiving rewards from others, and they didn't know about loyalty, commitment and concern for the other. Third, it is possible to teach more effective skills of conversation by education in the relevant principles.

The level at which conscious control takes over fluctuates: during training, clients are made unusually aware of turn-taking cues or gaze patterns, for example, though attention later passes to higher-level concerns. An important part of the social skill model is called "translation", the process of using feedback information to modify behaviour, for example, what to do if the other doesn't talk enough, becomes hostile, or presents some other problem? Some tests of social skill provide a sample of problems typical of the skill, to see how the client would cope with them. One method of SST is based on problem solving: trainees are taught how to tackle problem situations by thinking up solutions to scripted problems (Shure, 1981). Other methods of SST make use of educational methods, to increase knowledge and understanding of, for example social relationships, or behaviour in another culture.

Self-presentation

This is a special goal of social skill, which is important not only for the self-esteem of interactors, but also to enable others to know how to react. "Grey" or anonymous individuals are difficult to deal with. However, not all claims to identity or status are accepted, and each person's status and role in an encounter has to be negotiated and be acceptable to the others. Failures of skill are often due to failures in the sphere of self, resulting in undue self-consciousness and social anxiety.

The self-image is the whole set of thoughts that individuals have about themselves, including roles (job, social class, etc.), personality traits, and body image. Self-esteem is the extent to which individuals think well of themselves. Self-presentation is behaviour designed to influence the impressions of the self formed by others. Direct verbal claims to fame or status are usually laughed at and disbelieved in western culture, though indirect verbal forms are common ("as I was saying to X", etc.), as well as "face-work", such as excuses, apologies, and justifications to limit damage to face. Non-verbal self-presentation is probably more important: clothes and other aspects of appearance, accent and speech style, and general manner. Such signals can successfully create impressions of social class, group membership, personality, and political views. Self-presentation is often partly inflated, and Goffman (1956) predicted that if exposed this causes embarrassment. This prediction has been confirmed, though there are other sources of embarrassment, especially social accidents (e.g., forgetting someone's name), suddenly becoming the centre of attention, and inappropriate sexual events.

Embarrassment is part of social anxiety, which is partly the result of undue self-attention, and worry about social disapproval, leading to cautious and ineffective social performance (Froming, Corley, & Rinker, 1990). Actual or feared disapproval leads to low self-esteem, as does a gap between aspirations and achievements.

Self-disclosure of personal information is normally gradual and recipro-
cated, and is necessary for close relationships, as a sign of trust. Some
individuals spend a lot of time with friends, but still feel lonely, because the
conversation is not intimate enough (Jones, Hobbs, & Hockenbury, 1982).

Skills for different situations and relationships

The skills needed vary between different social situations. Some are commonly found difficult and are sources of anxiety: public performance, parties, dealing with depressed people, and conflict situations. Work involves a
number of standard situations: committees, presentations, interviews, negotiation, selling, and so on. These all require special moves, sequences and
physical settings, and are governed by rules about what should or should not
be done (Argyle et al., 1981).

Social relationships similarly need distinctive skills – for friends, spouses,
work subordinates, and others. Marriage requires a high level of rewardingness, for example, and the skills and willingness to negotiate and com-
promise. Again there are distinctive rules for each relationship. Many people
do not appear to understand relationships very well, so that there is scope for
an educational component to training. They may not realize the importance
of networks and third-party rules for friendship, or the number of decisions
to be made in marriage, from which conflict can very easily occur (Argyle &
Henderson, 1985).

INDIVIDUAL DIFFERENCES IN SOCIAL SKILLS

Gender

Men score higher on measures of assertiveness; the main demands for assertiveness training come from women. However, women score higher on most
of the other components of social competence; they score much higher on
empathy, and on measures of cooperativeness (Argyle, 1991). Women are
found to be more rewarding, they have better verbal skills (more fluent,
better grammar, more educated accents), and are more expressive non-
verbally (smile a lot more, gaze more, finer gestures). Male non-verbal behaviour reflects their assertiveness – louder voices, more interruptions, take up
more space (Argyle, 1988).

Age

All aspects of social skill increase with age, during childhood and adolescence. At student age many young people have difficulty making friends,
and with common social situations, though social competence improves

rapidly during this period (Bryant & Trower, 1974), and later as the result of having to cope with social tasks at work and in the family.

Social class

Studies of the social skills of children between 8 and 16 show that middle-class children do better on measures of taking the role of the other, reward-ingness, and social understanding, even with IQ held constant (e.g., Gollin, 1958). Middle-class adults do better on some aspects of skill, they are verbally more fluent, and take more account of the point of view of listeners. People in most middle-class jobs require more social skills, since most of them involve dealing with people and with complex social situations (e.g., doctors, lawyers, teachers, managers), compared with manual workers.

Personality

Intelligence is correlated with social intelligence and understanding, and probably with verbal skills. Extraverts are found more friendly and rewarding, and approach social situations in the confident expectation that they are going to get on well with people and enjoy themselves (Thorne, 1987). Argyle and Lu (1990a) found that they particularly enjoy two kinds of social situations – teams and clubs, dances and parties. Neuroticism is associated with social anxiety, lack of self-confidence, self-consciousness, and corresponding lack of social competence.

THE AETIOLOGY OF SOCIAL SKILLS

Social skills correlate with extraversion and intelligence, and negatively with neuroticism and other aspects of mental disorder, all of which are known to be partly inherited, so that there is probably an innate predisposition to become socially skilled, or the reverse.

Popularity and other aspects of social competence in children are caused by early warm relations with their mother, while unpopularity is caused by punitive and controlling styles of discipline and by stresses such as break-up of the family, and poverty (Ladd, 1991).

Parents influence the development of social skills throughout childhood in other ways. They provide models of assertiveness, sociability, cooperative-ness or lack of these, may encourage empathy, cooperation, or the reverse, and may coach and instruct, including such aspects of behaviour as "Look at me when I'm talking to you", "Don't interrupt", "Say hello". They may supervise play between siblings, and teach them to cooperate instead of quarrelling, and may provide peer-group contacts for their children.

Number and ages of siblings have rather complex effects on the develop-ment of social skills. First-born and only children are more independent, and surprisingly the more siblings a child has, the *lower* the child's subsequent extraversion (Eysenck & Cookson, 1970), probably because the child has less practice at sociability with peers outside the family. The skills learned depend on position in the family, so that girls with older brothers may learn indirect and skilful ways of out-witting them (Lamb & Sutton-Smith, 1982). Cooperative fantasy play takes place from an early age inside and outside the family, from 3 to 10, and children learn to follow rules, to see the point of view of others, to cooperate with peers, and in hierarchies, to inhibit aggression. This learning is partly by imitation, partly by trial and error (e.g., Howes, 1988).

Social skills continue to develop at school and at work. Young people learn to work under supervision, in a group, and to supervise others. They learn specialized skills such as committee chairmanship and public speaking. Trial and error is important, as is imitation, and special training courses.

Gender differences in social skill can be traced to childhood socialization. Many studies have shown how boys and girls are handled differently. Parents allow boys greater independence and encourage them to compete; parents are warmer towards girls, punish them less, and supervise them more closely (Huston, 1983). Generally boys model themselves on their fathers, girls on their mothers.

Failure of social competence in young adults can be traced to childhood experience, such as socially inadequate parents, geographical or other isolation, and little experience with the peer group. A study of American students found that socially inadequate male students often had similarly inadequate mothers (Sherman & Farina, 1974).

THE EFFECTS OF SOCIAL SKILLS

Social skills are important, because of the effects they have on relationships, and therefore on health and happiness, and on effectiveness at work. We shall discuss their effects on mental health later. Much of the research on this topic is in the form of correlations, or other statistical relationships, between social performance and such effects. This does not show causation, which requires experimental or longitudinal designs. There are some of these, and there is also research, which we report later, showing the effects of training in these skills.

Everyday life

We have listed the skills which lead to liking and popularity: rewardingness, positive non-verbal signals, following informal friendship rules, taking the role of the other, self-disclosure, and correct understanding of friendship. Rewardingness was first demonstrated by Jennings (1950). Sarason et al. (1985) found that the individuals who had difficulty finding social support were those who were unrewarding, introverted, pessimistic, alienated, intolerant, hostile, and had low self-esteem. Experimental studies have shown that people are liked more if they smile, have a friendly tone of voice, look more, and approach nearer (Argyle, 1988). There are a number of verbal techniques used by extraverts which may be very effective: agreeing, paying compliments, asking questions, finding things in common, use of first names, talking of pleasant events, and humour (Ellis & Beattie, 1986).

Marriage is the most important relationship, in terms of its effects on health and mental health, but about one-third of them fail. The social-skills sources of marital satisfaction include pleasing verbal acts and fewer criticisms, non-verbal acts (kiss, touch, presents, help), a problem solving approach to decisions, and a good sex life. Divorce and unhappy marriages, as judged by complaints, are in part caused by the following factors (Argyle & Henderson, 1985):

1 unfaithfulness
2 too little sex
3 arguing
4 lack of respect for spouse
5 not having interesting conversations
6 violence and drink.

Marital therapy focuses on training in rewardingness, and on negotiation. It would be useful to teach some of the informal rules too, such as faithfulness.

Many studies have shown the importance of social support for health (Schwarzer & Leppin, 1989). To obtain social support, social skills are needed to establish and maintain supportive relationships, especially with family, but also with friends and workmates. Social support leads to good health in several ways; close relationships like marriage produce greater immune system activity; positive emotions as produced by friends do the same; families look after each other, and encourage better health behaviour; and social support helps people cope with stress better, by practical help and emotional support (Sarason, Sarason, & Pierce, 1990).

Argyle and Lu (1990a) found that extraverts are happier than introverts, and in a longitudinal analysis found that this was partly because extraverts are more assertive and cooperative (Figure 2). The numbers are correlations. The top figure shows that extraversion predicts happiness with a correlation of .39, but that this effect is reduced to .28 when the effect of extraversion on assertiveness is taken into account. In another study it was found that extraverts are more cooperative in certain ways, and this too causes happiness at a later date (Lu & Argyle, 1991). A further process may be that extraverts send more positive non-verbal signals, they smile more, look more, and approach nearer, all of which are likely to produce a reciprocal response, and an elevated mood in both.

On the other hand lonely people (who are usually unhappy) suffer from social skills deficits: they are shy, unassertive, have social anxiety and low

A

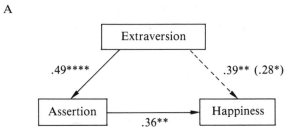

Figure 2a Assertiveness as a mediator of the extraversion–happiness relationship
Source: Argyle and Lu, 1990b

B

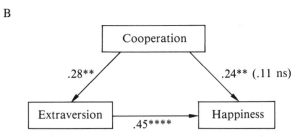

Figure 2b Extraversion as a mediator of the cooperation–happiness relationship
Source: Lu and Argyle, 1991

self-esteem, have negative and distrusting attitudes about relationships, and feel alienated (Jones, Hobbs, & Hockenbury, 1982).

Work effectiveness

Supervisory skills were the first to be studied, and it has often been shown that the productivity of work-groups is higher if supervisors use certain skills. These are a combination of initiating structure (giving instructions, etc.), consideration (looking after group members), and the democratic-persuasive style. There are modest effects on rate of work, greater if the work is not machine-paced, but much greater effects on absenteeism, job satisfaction, and labour turnover (see Figure 3).

These skills probably apply to all situations involving dealing with subordinates, especially groups of subordinates, in leisure groups as well as at work. However, there are also "contingencies", that is different skills are more important in different settings. For example if the task is unrewarding, more consideration is needed, if the best line of action is unclear, or if the group is unlikely to accept the leader's ideas, more participation is needed (Argyle, 1989).

91

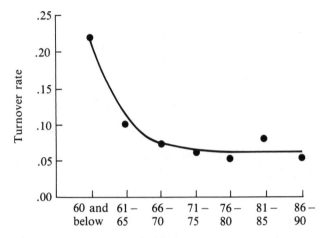

Figure 3a Effect of consideration on labour turnover
Source: Fleishman and Harris, 1962

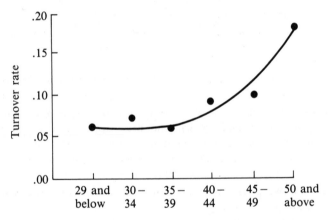

Figure 3b Effect of initiating structure on labour turnover
Source: Fleishman and Harris, 1962

Many studies have been made of school-teaching skills, and their effect on learning by pupils, and the results have been embodied in training courses. The most effective teaching style is a combination of a number of elements, including the businesslike organization of lessons, the use of examples and illustrations, questions, praise, and making use of pupil's ideas, as well as the usual leadership style (Rosenshine, 1971). Doctor skills are widely taught, but research has so far been directed only towards such sub-goals as accurate history-taking, patient satisfaction, and compliance with doctor's instructions, rather than with the health of patients (Maguire, 1986).

92

Cross-cultural skills are most important for working organizations, because of the very high "failure rate" described earlier. Critical incident surveys have analysed large numbers of instances where members of one culture have got into difficulties in a second culture, the correct skills discovered, and embodied in training texts known as Culture Assimilators (Fiedler, Mitchell, & Triandis, 1971).

SOCIAL SKILLS AND MENTAL HEALTH

Do mental patients have social skills deficits, and if so what kinds? Is lack of social skill a cause of mental disorder?

The social skills of mental patients

Individuals suffering from social anxiety or neuroticism are found to be less socially skilled in several ways. They speak less, and in particular initiate less conversation; they look less, smile less, have more speech disfluencies, and fidget more; they avoid social situations, especially those which they find difficult (e.g., parties, meeting strangers), and are less assertive; they expect that social events will have negative outcomes. These are general findings; there are some socially anxious and neurotic patients who have normal social skills (Trower, 1986).

Depressives have been found to differ from other people in non-verbal style: more depressed faces, less gaze, less proximity, more self-touching gestures, drooping postures, a speech style which is lacking in vitality (low and falling pitch, slow and weak), and drab appearance (Argyle, 1988). However, these deficits are not found in all depressives, and more global effects are more characteristic. Depressives alienate other people quickly, and are avoided; they talk little, mainly about themselves, are unassertive, and above all are unrewarding: this may result in their becoming socially isolated (Williams, 1986).

More than other disorders schizophrenia covers a wide range of patients. However, comparisons of schizophrenics and controls have often found differences in non-verbal communication: schizophrenics show less facial expression but with some grimaces, avert gaze when talking to psychologists about their problems, need a great deal of personal space, direct gestures mainly to themselves, their voices tend to be silent, monotonous, of low volume and flat, they fail to synchronize speech and gesture, or coordinate their behaviour with that of others, and their appearance is characteristically odd and eccentric (Argyle, 1988). Their conversation is incoherent and unresponsive, they form very weak relationships or none, do not like being supervised, and are upset by criticism (Williams, 1986).

93

Delinquents are rated as less socially competent, have lower levels of gaze and smiling, and fidget more than non-delinquent controls. They do less well on tests of how to cope with social situations, especially at dealing with adults in authority, and they suggest aggressive rather than more skilled solutions to problem situations (Henderson & Hollin, 1986). Some violent criminals are overcontrolled and unassertive; some sexual offenders lack heterosexual skills. It seems likely that social skills failure is at least part of the cause of antisocial behaviour in these cases (Howells, 1986).

Psychopaths are different: they are not lacking in social skills, indeed they can be charming and persuasive when it suits them. What they lack is affection for or empathy with other people; they are very impulsive and lack the usual restraints on aggression or sexuality.

Explanations of the link between social skills deficits and mental disorder

First, skills deficits may cause mental disorder. Trower et al. (1978) proposed that, as a result of faulty socialization, some young people become socially unskilled; this leads to rejection and social isolation, which in turn result in depression and anxiety. A similar theory was put forward by Libet and Lewinsohn (1973), who found that depressives are very unrewarding to others; they argue that as a result others avoid them, and they then receive few rewards.

Second, the Sarasons' social support version: Sarason et al. (1985) found that individuals with poor social skills are less likely to be able to establish socially supportive relationships, and are therefore more likely to be upset by stress. Many studies have shown the importance of social support for good mental health, from Brown and Harris (1978) onwards. It is important to be loved, and to be accepted as part of a social network, in order to enjoy companionship, find emotional support, and receive serious help.

The third explanation is that the real cause is anxiety, neuroticism, and so on: certain personalities are predisposed both to mental disorder and to inadequate social behaviour. Henderson, Byrne, and Duncan-Jones (1981) found that neuroticism predicted both lack of social support and mental disorder. They have found that treating socially inadequate patients by desensitization improved both their mental health and their social skills, suggesting that anxiety may have been the real cause. Schizophrenics have inadequate social skills but this may be the result of more fundamental personality disturbance. However, it would still be possible for poor social skills to cause further problems and result in amplification of symptoms.

SOCIAL SKILLS TRAINING: HOW IT IS DONE

The classical method

There are three or four phases:

1 explanation and modelling, live or from video
2 role-playing with other trainees or stooges
3 comments from trainer and playback of videotape
4 repeat performance.

This is typically carried out in groups of six, for one to one-and-a-half hours, once or twice a week. The full package includes all the above features, and the groups may be supplemented by individual sessions. Modelling is an important component of role-playing, that is, showing how the skill should be done. This can be on videotape. There can be more than one example and these should not be too perfectly done. Figure 4 shows arrangements for a social skills training laboratory, with one-way screen, video cameras, and an ear microphone to instruct a trainee during the role-playing.

There may be six, ten, or more sessions. A serious problem is how to achieve generalization to real-life situations. For those not resident in

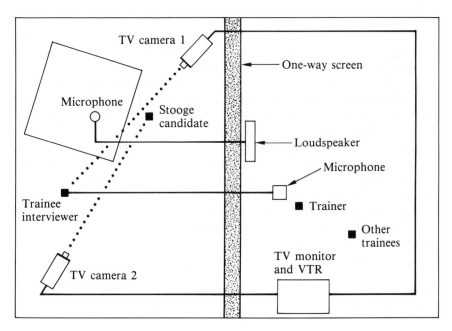

Figure 4 Social skills training laboratory
Source: Argyle, 1983

institutions "homework" is often used: trainees are asked to repeat the exercises (e.g., to make someone else talk more, or less) between sessions in real-life settings, and to report back. For those in hospital or prison, other staff can continue the training between the formal sessions.

Role-playing can deal with a wide range of skills and problems. For example exercises can focus on social relationships, or on situations which are found difficult.

Other laboratory methods

Role-playing is not the best way of training all of the components of social skills which have been described. Sending non-verbal signals, by face and voice, is most effectively trained by simple exercises with mirrors, video and audio-tape recorders. Failures of self-presentation are quite easily dealt with by changes of appearance, and sometimes voice training. Conversational failures may need some instruction on the conduct of conversations, and simple exercises, which may include role-played interviewing. Failure to take the role of the other can be tackled in various ways, including exercises in finding out the opinions of others.

Educational methods

Lecture and discussion methods were abandoned long ago as methods of SST when they were found to be ineffective, and because it is obvious that motor skills cannot be learned in this way. However, various research studies should make us think again. The Culture Assimilator, for inter-cultural training, has been quite successful (see Fiedler et al., 1971); books on assertiveness have been very popular. Our research on rules suggests another area where straightforward instruction is indicated. Much trouble with relationships arises because of misunderstanding the nature of friendship, marriage, and so on. Conversational skills involve some understanding of the principles of conversational structure. In all these cases direct teaching may be the best method. It is particularly important to learn the informal rules of situations and relationships. However, there is more to the performance of skills than knowing the rules, and behavioural practice is necessary too.

Learning on the job

For some jobs it is not possible to create role-play situations which simulate the work situation at all realistically. Police dealing with ethnic situations or managers dealing with trade unions are examples. An alternative to role-playing exercises in the lab is coaching on the job, starting with easy situations, by a trainer who accompanies the trainee and gives immediate coaching and feedback. This has long been done for schoolteachers, and is now done in some areas for police by "tutor constables".

Design of work skills courses

Some preliminary research is needed to discover what the problems are in the situations which, for example, police officers or supervisors find difficult. This could be done by surveys of potential trainees, or of experienced practitioners, or of their clients and subordinates. An example is a critical incident survey of people who have got into difficulty working in another country. Table 2 shows the skills taught on some American supervisory courses.

Table 2 List of skills taught to supervisors on some American courses

1 Orienting a new employee
2 Giving recognition
3 Motivating a poor employee
4 Correcting poor work habits
5 Discussing potential disciplinary action
6 Reducing absenteeism
7 Handling a complaining employee
8 Reducing turnover
9 Overcoming resistance to change

Source: Latham and Saari, 1979

It is then necessary to decide which are the best skills for dealing with these problems, by drawing on relevant research, or seeking the advice of those with a lot of experience of the job, though they can sometimes be wrong. A training course can then be devised to train employees in the approved ways of dealing with the problem situations. This will normally be based on role-playing in groups, but can include training on the job, and some educational input from lectures and discussion.

Design of SST for individual patients

A patient's social behaviour first needs to be carefully assessed by role-playing exercises, interview and questionnaire (described above). The patient can attend a number of role-played training sessions with other patients who have similar needs, such as for basic social skills. Other patients can act as the stooges. The patient can then be given a few individual sessions, to deal with any more idiosyncratic problems, for example, particular social situations that present difficulties. At either stage the training can include laboratory methods other than role-playing, such as non-verbal exercises. At the

97

end of each session the patient can be given written notes about what to think about, and instructions for homework.

SOCIAL SKILLS TRAINING: DOES IT WORK?

For the general population

SST is needed by, and to a small extent provided for, all age-groups. However, adolescents and young adults are the group for whom the need appears to be greatest, and where a high rate of success is reported. There are four main varieties.

Assertiveness courses have been found to be very effective, in before-and-after studies, sometimes using realistic but rather unethical role-play tasks with annoying confederates. Compared with anxiety reduction and cognitive therapy, assertiveness training and other SST have more effect on behaviour, though similar effects on feelings of anxiety and anger.

Heterosexual skills training, mostly with American students, has also been very successful, for example, in terms of number of dates per week, anxiety, and behavioural measures of skill. It is not clear whether improved skills or anxiety reduction are more important; some success has been obtained from simply arranging practice dates, without further training.

Loneliness is mainly caused by social isolation, due to poor social skills, and is common among young people. In extreme cases it is a cause of mental disorder. Training in the skills needed is straightforward and very successful (Furnham, 1986).

Adults of all ages have social skills needs too. One of the greatest is for marital therapy. Positive benefits for 65 per cent of clients are reported for SST focusing on rewardingness, improved communication, and negotiation skills (Argyle & Henderson, 1985).

Work skills

Most jobs require social skills, and most people pick these up by doing them. However, some fail completely and give up, for example many teachers, while others are very ineffective. Follow-up studies have used before-and-after comparisons of SST to find the effect on objective measures or on rated competence or rated social performance.

Managers, supervisors, and leaders of all kinds can be trained successfully, in terms of the effects on productivity, sales, etc., and of the job satisfaction and absenteeism of their subordinates (Burke & Day, 1986). Most firms use some kind of SST for this.

About 80 per cent of British teachers receive some "microteaching", with small classes; all aspects of teaching skills can be improved, including the elimination of errors, both for beginners and the experienced (Brown & Shaw, 1986).

Mental patients

There have been many experimental studies of the effectiveness of SST. The usual design is before-and-after comparisons of patients who are given SST, compared with others on a waiting list or who are given other kinds of treatment. Assessments are made of clinical conditions, social skills (e.g., by role-play measures), and subjective discomfort. Shepherd carried out an analysis of 52 such studies with adult psychiatric patients (Spence & Shepherd, 1983); reviews of follow-up studies of different kinds of patients are given in Hollin and Trower (1986). The conclusions of this research are as follows:

1 SST is better than no treatment, or placebo treatment, for all kinds of patients.
2 It is usually no better than the best alternative treatments, such as desensitization, cognitive therapy, or drugs.
3 However, it does have more effect on social skills.
4 It is the best treatment for neurotics who are socially unskilled or anxious.
5 Outcomes are improved if SST is added to other treatments, e.g., for schizophrenics.
6 It is not clear that improved social skills are always the cause of improvement; other treatments for depression have sometimes led to improved social behaviour as part of general recovery.

CONCLUSIONS

1 Social skills are patterns of social behaviour which make people competent in social situations. They can be assessed by role-playing, interviews, ratings by others, or objective results. There are many questionnaire measures but none has so far been widely accepted.
2 Many people suffer from inadequate social skills, especially adolescents and young adults, most mental patients, and a lot of people at work.
3 Social skills are like motor skills in their hierarchical structure and rapid response to feedback; assertiveness and rewardingness are important components, as are the verbal and non-verbal elements, empathy and cooperation, problem solving and understanding, self-presentation, and the skills for different situations and relationships.
4 There are individual differences in the social skills of men and women, different social classes, and personalities.
5 Social skills are mainly acquired from experience in the family and peer groups, and later at work.

6 Social skills have massive effects on popularity, marriage and other relationships, health and happiness, and effectiveness at work.

7 Most mental patients and many offenders have defective social skills, and for some of them this is a cause of their trouble.

8 SST is usually done by role-playing, but can be supplemented by other laboratory methods, educational methods, and training on the job. It is very effective with non-patients, is as good as alternative methods for many kinds of patients, or can be a supplement to them, and is effective for a wide range of work skills.

FURTHER READING

Hollin, C. R., & Trower, P. (Eds) (1986). *Handbook of social skills training* (2 vols). Oxford: Pergamon.

L'Abate, L., & Milan, M. A. (Eds) (1985). *Handbook of social skills training and research*. New York: Wiley.

Spence, S., & Shepherd, G. (1983). *Developments in social skills training*. London: Academic Press.

Trower, P., Bryant, B., & Argyle, M. (1978). *Social skills and mental health*. London: Methuen.

Wine, J. D., & Smye, M. D. (Eds) (1981). *Social competence*. New York: Guilford.

REFERENCES

Argyle, M. (1983). *The psychology of interpersonal behaviour*, 4th edn. Harmondsworth: Penguin.

Argyle, M. (1984). Some new developments in social skills training. *Bulletin of the British Psychological Society*, *37*, 405–410.

Argyle, M. (1988). *Bodily communication*, 2nd edn. London: Methuen.

Argyle, M. (1989). *The social psychology of work*, 2nd edn. Harmondsworth: Penguin.

Argyle, M. (1991). *Cooperation: The basis of sociability*. London: Routledge.

Argyle, M., Furnham, A., & Graham, J. A. (1981). *Social situations*. Cambridge: Cambridge University Press.

Argyle, M., & Henderson, M. (1985). *The anatomy of relationships*. London: Heinemann, and Harmondsworth: Penguin.

Argyle, M., & Lu, L. (1990a). The happiness of extraverts. *Personality and Individual Differences*, *11*, 1011–1017.

Argyle, M., & Lu, L. (1990b). Happiness and social skills. *Personality and Individual Differences*, *11*, 1255–1261.

Argyle, M., Henderson, M., & Furnham, A. (1985). The rules of social relationships. *British Journal of Social Psychology*, *24*, 125–129.

Brown, G., & Harris, T. (1978). *Social origins of depression*. London: Tavistock.

Brown, G., & Shaw, M. (1986). Social skills training in education. In C. R. Hollin & P. Trower (Eds) *Handbook of social skills training* (vol. 1, pp. 59–78). Oxford: Pergamon.

Bryant, B., & Trower, P. (1974). Social difficulty in a student population. *British Journal of Educational Psychology*, *44*, 13–24.

Bryant, B., Trower, P., Yardley, K., Urbieta, H., & Letemendia, F. (1976). A survey of social inadequacy among psychiatric patients. *Psychological Medicine*, *6*, 101–112.

Bull, R., & Horncastle, P. (1983). *An evaluation of the Metropolitan Police recruit training programme*. London: Police Foundation.

Burke, M. J., & Day, R. R. (1986). A cumulative study of the effectiveness of management training. *Journal of Applied Psychology*, *71*, 232–245.

Dodge, K. A. (no date). *Cooperation in children*. Unpublished manuscript, University of Indiana.

Eisenberg, N., & Strayer, J. (Eds) (1987). *Empathy and its development*. Cambridge: Cambridge University Press.

Ellis, A., & Beattie, G. (1986). *The psychology of language and communication*. London: Weidenfeld & Nicolson.

Eysenck, H. J., & Cookson, D. (1970). Personality in primary school children: 3. Family background. *British Journal of Educational Psychology*, *40*, 117–131.

Fiedler, F. E., Mitchell, R., & Triandis, H. C. (1971). The culture assimilator: An approach to cross-cultural training. *Journal of Applied Psychology*, *55*, 95–102.

Flanders, N. A. (1970). *Analyzing teaching behavior*. Reading, MA: Addison-Wesley.

Fleishman, E. A. (1953). The description of supervisory behavior. *Journal of Applied Psychology*, *37*, 1–6.

Fleishman, E. A., & Harris, E. F. (1962). Patterns of leadership behavior related to employee grievances and turnover. *Journal of Occupational Psychology*, *53*, 65–72.

Friedman, H. S., Prince, L. M., Riggio, R. E., & DiMatteo, M. R. (1980). Understanding and assessing non-verbal expressiveness: The affective communication test. *Journal of Personality and Social Psychology*, *39*, 333–351.

Froming, W. J., Corley, E. B., & Rinker, L. (1990). The influence of public self consciousness and the audience's characteristics on withdrawal from embarrassing situations. *Journal of Personality*, *58*, 603–622.

Furnham, A. (1986). Social skills training with adolescents and young adults. In C. R. Hollin & P. Trower (Eds) *Handbook of social skills training* (vol. 1, pp. 33–57). Oxford: Pergamon.

Galassi, J. P., Galassi, M. D., & Vedder, M. J. (1981). Perspectives on assertion as a social skills model. In J. D. Wine & M. D. Smye (Eds) *Social competence* (pp. 287–345). New York: Guilford.

Giles, H., & Coupland, N. (1991). *Language: Contexts and consequences*. Milton Keynes: Open University Press.

Goffman, E. (1956). *The presentation of self in everyday life*. Edinburgh: Edinburgh University Press.

Gollin, E. S. (1958). Organizational characteristics of social judgment: A developmental investigation. *Journal of Personality*, *26*, 139–154.

Grice, H. P. (1975). Logic and conversation. In P. Cole & J. Morgan (Eds) *Syntax and semiotics: Speech acts*. New York and London: Academic Press. (vol. 3, pp. 41–58).

Hargie, O., Saunders, S., & Dickson, D. (1987). *Social skills in interpersonal communication*, 2nd edn. London: Routledge.

Hays, R. B. (1988). Friendship. In S. W. Duck (Ed.) *Handbook of personal relationships* (pp. 391–408). Chichester: Wiley.

Henderson, M., & Hollin, C. R. (1986). Social skills training and delinquency. In C. R. Hollin & P. Trower (Eds) *Handbook of social skills training* (vol. 1, pp. 79–101). Oxford: Pergamon.

Henderson, S., Byrne, D. G., & Duncan-Jones, P. (1981). *Neurosis and the social environment*. Sydney: Academic Press.

Hochschild, A. R. (1983). *The managed heart*. Berkeley, CA: University of California Press.

Hollin, C. R., & Trower, P. (Eds) (1986). *Handbook of social skills training* (2 vols). Oxford: Pergamon.

Howells, K. (1986), Social skills training and criminal and antisocial behaviour. In C. R. Hollin and P. Trower (Eds) *Handbook of social skills training* (vol. 1, pp. 185–210). Oxford: Pergamon.

Howes, C. (1988). Peer interaction of young children. *Monographs of Society for Research in Child Development*, *53*, no. 1.

Huston, A. C. (1983). Sex-typing. In P. H. Musson & E. M. Hetherington (Eds) *Handbook of child psychology* (vol. 4, pp. 387–467). New York: Wiley.

Ingram, R. E. (1989). Self-focused attention in clinical disorders: Review and a conceptual model. *Psychological Bulletin*, *107*, 156–176.

Jennings, H. H. (1950). *Leadership and isolation*. New York: Longman Green.

Jones, W. H., Hobbs, S. A., & Hockenbury, D. (1982). Loneliness and social skills deficits. *Journal of Personality and Social Psychology*, *42*, 682–689.

Ladd, G. W. (1991). Family–peer relationships. Special issue of *Journal of Social and Personal Relationships*, *3*.

La Gaipa, J. J., & Wood, H. D. (1981). Friendship in disturbed adolescents. In S. Duck & R. Gilmour (Eds) *Personal relationships: Personal relationships in disorder* (vol. 3, pp. 169–189). London: Academic Press.

Lamb, M. E., & Sutton-Smith, B. (1982). *Sibling relationships*. Hillsdale, NJ: Lawrence Erlbaum.

Latham, G. P., & Saari, L. M. (1979). Application of social-learning theory to training supervisors through behavioral modelling. *Journal of Applied Psychology*, *64*, 239–246.

Lazarus, A. A. (1973). On assertive behavior: A brief note. *Behavior Therapy*, *4*, 697–699.

Libet, J., & Lewinsohn, P. M. (1973). The concept of social skill with special reference to the behavior of depressed persons. *Journal of Consulting and Clinical Psychology*, *40*, 304–312.

Linde, C. (1988). The quantification study of communication success: Politeness and accidents in aviation discourse. *Language in Society*, *17*, 375–399.

Lu, L., & Argyle, M. (1991). Happiness and cooperation. *Personality and Individual Differences*, *12*, 1019–1030.

McNamara, J. R., & Blumer, C. A. (1982). Role playing to assess social competence: Ecological validity considerations. *Behavior Modification 6*, 519–549.

Maguire, P. (1986). Social skills training for health professional. In C. R. Hollin & P. Trower (Eds) *Handbook of social skills training* (vol. 2, pp. 143–165). Oxford: Pergamon.

Mehrabian, A., & Epstein, N. (1972), A measure of emotional empathy. *Journal of Personality*, *40*, 525–543.

Muchinsky, P. M. (1986). Personnel selection methods. In C. L. Cooper & I. T. Robertson (Eds) *International review of industrial and organizational psychology* (pp. 37–70). Chichester: Wiley.

Nisbett, R. E., & Wilson, T. D. (1977). Telling more than we know: Verbal reports on mental processes. *Psychological Review*, *84*, 231–259.

Rathus, S. A. (1973). A 30-item schedule for assessing assertive behavior. *Behavior Therapy*, *4*, 398–406.

Rosenshine, B. (1971). *Teaching behaviours and student achievement.* Slough: National Foundation for Educational Research.

Rosenthal, R., Hall, J. A., DiMatteo, M. R., Rogers, P. L., & Archer, D. (1979). *Sensitivity to nonverbal communication in the PONS test.* Baltimore, MD: Johns Hopkins University Press.

Sarason, B. R., Sarason, I. G., Hacker, T. A., & Basham, R. B. (1985). Concomitants of social support: Social skills, physical attractiveness, and gender. *Journal of Personality and Social Psychology, 49,* 469–480.

Sarason, B. R., Sarason, I. G., & Pierce, G. R. (Eds) (1990). *Social support: An interactional view.* Chichester: Wiley.

Schwarzer, R., & Leppin, A. (1989). Social support and health: A meta-analysis. *Psychology and Health, 3,* 1–15.

Shepherd, G. (1986). Social skills training and schizophrenia. In C. R. Hollin & P. Trower (Eds) *Handbook of social skills training* (vol. 2, pp. 9–37). Oxford: Pergamon.

Sherman, H., & Farina, A. (1974). Social adequacy of parents and children. *Journal of Abnormal Psychology, 83,* 327–330.

Shure, M. B. (1981). Social competence as a problem-solving skill. In J. D. Wine & M. D. Smye (Eds) *Social competence* (pp. 158–185). New York: Guilford.

Spence, S., & Shepherd, G. (1983). *Developments in social skills training.* London: Academic Press.

Spitzberg, B. H., & Cupach, W. R. (1989). *Handbook of interpersonal competence research.* New York: Springer.

Thorne, A. (1987). A press of personality: A study of conversation between introverts and extraverts. *Journal of Personality and Social Psychology, 53,* 718–726.

Trower, P. (1986) Social skills training and social anxiety. In C. R. Hollin & P. Trower (Eds) *Handbook of social skills training* (vol. 2, pp. 39–65). Oxford: Pergamon.

Trower, P., Bryant, B., & Argyle, M. (1978). *Social skills and mental health.* London: Methuen.

Williams, J. M. G. (1986). Social skills training and depression. In C. R. Hollin & P. Trower (Eds) *Handbook of social skills training* (vol. 2, pp. 91–110). Oxford: Pergamon.

GLOSSARY

This glossary is confined to a selection of frequently used terms that merit explanation or comment. Its informal definitions are intended as practical guides to meanings and usages. The entries are arranged alphabetically, word by word, and numerals are positioned as though they were spelled out.

accommodation 1. in Piaget's theory of cognitive development, the type of adaptation in which old cognitive schemata (q.v.) are modified or new ones formed in order to absorb information that can neither be ignored nor adapted through assimilation (q.v.) into the existing network of knowledge, beliefs, and expectations. **2.** In vision, modification of the shape of the eye's lens to focus on objects at different distances. **3.** In social psychology, the modification of behaviour in response to social pressure or group norms, as for example in conformity.

adolescence from the Latin *adolescere*, to grow up, the period of development between puberty and adulthood.

applied behaviour analysis the application of learning theory to behavioural problems in everyday settings, including hospitals, clinics, schools, and factories. Research and practice in this field is described by its practitioners as applied, behavioural, analytic, technological, conceptually systematic, effective, and capable of generalized effects. *See also* behaviour modification.

aptitude tests tests designed to measure people's potential abilities or capacities for acquiring various types of skills or knowledge.

arousal a general term for an organism's state of physiological activation, mediated by the autonomic nervous system. *See also* Yerkes-Dodson law.

assimilation the process of absorbing new information into existing cognitive structures and modifying it as necessary to fit with existing structures. In Piaget's theory of cognitive development, the type of adaptation in which existing cognitive schemata (q.v.) select for incorporation only those items of information that fit or can be forced into the existing network of knowledge, beliefs, and expectations. *Cf.* accommodation.

association areas parts of the cerebral cortex (q.v.) not primarily devoted to sensory or motor functions.

autonomic nervous system a subdivision of the nervous system that regulates (autonomously) the internal organs and glands. It is divided into the sympathetic nervous system and the parasympathetic nervous system.

avoidance conditioning a form of operant conditioning (q.v.) in which, in order to avoid an aversive stimulus, the animal or person being conditioned must learn to make some evasive response.

behaviour modification the application of techniques of operant conditioning (q.v.)

105

to reduce or eliminate maladaptive or problematic behaviour patterns or to develop new ones. *See also* applied behaviour analysis, cognitive-behaviour therapy, flooding.

behaviour therapy a therapeutic technique based on the principles of conditioning and behaviour modification (qq.v.).

behaviourism a school of psychology founded by John B. Watson in 1913 which considers objectively observed behaviour rather than inner mental experiences to be the proper subject for study. Behaviourists tend to stress the importance of the environment as a determinant of human and animal behaviour.

cerebellum from the Latin diminutive form of *cerebrum*, brain, one of the main divisions of the brain, situated beneath the back of the main part of the brain, involved in the regulation of movement and balance.

cerebral cortex from the Latin *cerebrum*, brain, *cortex*, bark, the thin layer of cells covering the cerebrum (q.v.), largely responsible for higher mental functions.

cerebrum from the Latin word meaning brain, the largest brain structure, comprising the front and upper part of the brain, of which the cortex (outer layer) controls most sensory, motor, and cognitive processes in human beings.

choice reaction time *see under* reaction time.

chunking the tendency to organize small items of information into larger meaningful units or 'chunks' as, for example, when a skilled reader takes in whole words or phrases at a glance without noticing individual letters separately or when an accomplished musical sight reader processes several bars of music as a single chunk.

classical (Pavlovian) conditioning the process, first described by the Nobel Prize-winning Russian physiologist Ivan Petrovich Pavlov, sometimes called respondent conditioning, by which an initially neutral stimulus acquires the capacity to elicit a response through association with a stimulus that naturally elicits that response. *Cf.* operant conditioning.

cognition from the Latin *cognoscere*, to know, attention, thinking, problem-solving, remembering, and all other mental processes that fall under the general heading of information processing.

cognitive-behaviour therapy techniques of psychotherapy based on methods of behaviour modification (q.v.) with an emphasis on the learning of cognitive responses involving imagery, fantasy, thoughts, and above all beliefs.

cognitive psychology the branch of psychology devoted to the study of attention, memory, imagery, perception, language, thinking and problem solving, artificial intelligence (AI), and generally all mental operations that involve information processing.

cognitive schema (pl. schemata or schemas) an integrated network of knowledge, beliefs, and expectations relating to a particular subject; in Piaget's theory of cognitive development, the basic element of mental life.

cognitive skills acquired proficiencies at information processing tasks, for example mathematics or games such as chess, whose perceptual and motor requirements are not significant. *Cf.* motor skills, social skills.

conditioning *see* classical (Pavlovian) conditioning, operant conditioning.

continuous reinforcement in learning theory, a schedule of reinforcement (q.v.) in which every response is reinforced. *Cf.* intermittent (partial) reinforcement.

control group in experimental design, a comparison group of subjects who are not exposed to the treatment that subjects in the experimental group are exposed to, but who in other respects are treated identically, to provide a baseline against which to evaluate the effects of the treatment.

convergent thinking thinking characterized by synthesis of information, especially in the course of arriving at a unique solution to a problem; analytical, usually deductive thinking in which formal rules are followed, as in arithmetic. *Cf.* divergent thinking.

correlation in statistics, the relationship between two variables such that high scores on one tend to go with high scores on the other or (in the case of negative correlation) such that high scores on one tend to go with low scores on the other. The usual index of correlation, called the product-moment correlation coefficient and symbolized by r, ranges from 1.00 for perfect positive correlation, through zero for uncorrelated variables, to −1.00 for perfect negative correlation.

critical period a biologically determined stage of development at which a person or animal is optimally ready to acquire some pattern of behaviour. *See also* imprinting.

delusion a false personal belief, maintained in the face of overwhelming contradictory evidence, excluding religious beliefs that are widely accepted by members of the person's culture or sub-culture, characteristic especially of delusional (paranoid) disorder. *Cf.* hallucination.

depression a sustained negative mood state characterized by sadness, pessimism, a general feeling of despondency, passivity, indecisiveness, suicidal thoughts, sleep disturbances, and other mental and physical symptoms, associated with some mood disorders.

divergent thinking imaginative thinking characterized by the generation of multiple possible solutions to a problem, often associated with creativity. *Cf.* convergent thinking.

DSM-IV the common name of the fourth edition of the *Diagnostic and Statistical Manual of Mental Disorders* of the American Psychiatric Association, published in 1994, replacing DSM-III-R, the revised version of the third edition published in 1987, containing the most authoritative classification and definitions of mental disorders.

electroencephalogram (EEG) from the Greek *electron*, amber (in which electricity was first observed), *en*, in, *kephale*, head, *gramme*, line, a visual record of the electrical activity of the brain, recorded via electrodes attached to the scalp. The recording apparatus is called an electroencephalograph.

emotion from the Latin *e*, away, *movere*, to move, any evaluative, affective, intentional, short-term psychological state.

ethology from the Greek *ethos*, character, *logos*, study, the study of the behaviour of animals in their natural habitats.

evoked potential a characteristic pattern in an electroencephalogram (EEG) (q.v.) in response to a specific stimulus.

extinction in classical conditioning, the repeated presentation of a conditional stimulus without its associated unconditional stimulus, which leads in certain circumstances to the gradual elimination of the conditional (conditioned) response; in operant conditioning (q.v.), a process whereby the relative frequency of a learned response decreases when reinforcement is withdrawn.

fixed interval (FI) schedule *see under* schedules of reinforcement.

fixed ratio (FR) schedule *see under* schedules of reinforcement.

flooding a technique of behaviour therapy (q.v.) for treating phobias (q.v.) in which the client is exposed to the phobic stimulus for extended periods of time without the opportunity of escape.

hallucination from the Latin *alucinari*, to wander in the mind, a false perception, most commonly visual or auditory, subjectively similar or identical to an ordinary perception but occurring in the absence of relevant sensory stimuli, characteristic in particular of some forms of schizophrenia. False perceptions occurring during sleep, while falling asleep (hypnagogic image), or while awakening (hypnopompic image) are not normally considered to be hallucinations. *Cf.* delusion.

hippocampus from the Greek *hippos*, horse, *kampos*, sea monster, a structure in the brain, whose cross section has the shape of a sea horse, involved in emotion, motivation, learning, and the establishment of long-term memory.

hypothalamus a pea-sized structure situated (as its name indicates) below the thalamus at the base of the brain, crucially involved in the regulation of the autonomic nervous system (q.v.) and the control of temperature, heart-rate, blood pressure, hunger, thirst, and sexual arousal.

imprinting in ethology (q.v.), a form of rapid learning that takes place during a critical period (q.v.) of development and is extremely resistant to extinction (q.v.). The most familiar example is the behaviour of newly hatched ducklings, which will become imprinted on, and subsequently follow around, virtually any moving object that is presented during this critical period.

instrumental conditioning *see* operant conditioning.

interference *see under* proactive interference (PI), retroactive interference (RI).

intermittent (partial) reinforcement in learning theory, any schedule of reinforcement (q.v.) in which not all responses are reinforced. *Cf.* continuous reinforcement.

kinaesthesis from the Greek *kinein*, to move, *aisthesis*, feeling, the sensory modality, also called muscle sense, through which bodily position, weight, muscle tension, and movement are perceived.

law of effect a law first propounded by the American psychologist Edward Thorndike in 1904 stating that any behaviour followed by reward is more likely to occur in the future.

learning the relatively permanent change in behaviour that occurs as a result of experience. *See also* operant conditioning.

limbic system a ring of structures surrounding the brain stem concerned with emotion, hunger, and sex.

long-term memory (LTM) relatively long-lasting memory for information that has been deeply processed. *Cf.* sensory memory, short-term memory (STM).

memory the mental processes of encoding, storage, and retrieval of information. *See also* long-term memory, sensory memory, short-term memory (STM).

mental disorder according to DSM-IV (q.v.), a psychological or behavioural syndrome or pattern associated with distress (a painful symptom), disability (impairment in one or more areas of functioning), and a significantly increased risk of death, pain, disability, or an important loss of freedom, occurring not merely as a predictable response to a disturbing life-event.

motivation the motive forces responsible for the initiation, persistence, direction, and vigour of goal-directed behaviour.

motor skills acquired proficiencies at tasks requiring complex bodily movements or physical coordination. *Cf.* cognitive skills, social skills.

multiple personality disorder a rare dissociative disorder in which two or more markedly different personalities coexist within the same individual, popularly confused with schizophrenia (q.v.).

muscle sense *see* kinaesthesis.

negative reinforcement reinforcement (q.v.) that results from the removal rather than the presentation of the reinforcer (which, by implication, is an aversive or punishing negative reinforcer). *Cf.* positive reinforcement.

non-verbal communication the collective name for all forms of communication apart from spoken or written language, including the communicative effects of vocal quality, facial expression, postures, and gestures.

observational learning *see* vicarious learning.

operant conditioning a type of learning, sometimes called instrumental conditioning, which focuses on the process by which behaviour changes as a result of its consequences, in particular the way in which an individual's behavioural responses become more or less frequent as a consequence of reinforcement (q.v.).

partial reinforcement *see* intermittent (partial) reinforcement.

phobia from the Greek *phobos*, fear, an irrational, debilitating, persistent, and intense fear of a specific type of object, activity, or situation, which, if certain diagnostic criteria are fulfilled, may be considered a mental disorder (q.v.).

placebo from the Latin word meaning I shall please (the opening words of the Roman Catholic office or service for the dead are *Placebo Domino*, I shall please the Lord), an inactive substance or dummy treatment administered to a control group (q.v.) to compare its effects with those of a real drug or treatment.

positive reinforcement a process of reinforcement (q.v.) in which the relative frequency of the response is increased by the presentation of a reinforcer with rewarding properties. *Cf.* negative reinforcement.

proactive interference (PI) the inhibitory effect of information learned in the past on the learning of new information, especially noticeable when the two sets of material are very similar. *Cf.* retroactive interference (RI).

psychology from the Greek *psyche*, mind, *logos*, study, the study of the nature, functions, and phenomena of behaviour and mental experience.

reaction time the minimum time between the presentation of a stimulus and a subject's response. In experiments involving choice reaction time, the subject is presented at unpredictable times with one of two or more stimuli, each of which requires a different response.

reinforcement in learning theory, the strengthening of the bond between a stimulus and a response (qq.v.) or anything that increases the relative frequency of a response. *See also* continuous reinforcement, intermittent (partial) reinforcement, negative reinforcement, positive reinforcement, reinforcer, schedules of reinforcement.

reinforcer any stimulus or event that increases the relative frequency of a response during the process of reinforcement (q.v.).

response any behavioural or glandular activity of a person or an animal, especially as a reaction to a stimulus (q.v.).

retroactive interference (RI) the inhibiting effect that the learning of new information has on the recall of material learned previously, especially when the two sets of material are very similar. *Cf.* proactive interference (PI).

schedules of reinforcement in operant conditioning (q.v.), a rule describing the functional relationship between reinforcement (q.v.) and an organism's responses. In a fixed ratio (FR) schedule, reinforcement occurs regularly after a fixed number of responses; in a fixed interval (FI) schedule, reinforcement occurs after fixed intervals irrespective of the organism's responses; variable ratio (VR) and variable interval (VI) schedules are defined *mutatis mutandis*.

schizophrenia from the Greek *schizein*, to split, *phren*, mind, a group of mental disorders characterized by incoherent thought and speech, hallucinations (q.v.), delusions (q.v.), flattened or inappropriate affect, deterioration of social functioning, and lack of self-care. In spite of its derivation, the word does not refer to multiple personality disorder (q.v.).

sensory memory a form of memory, necessary for normal vision and hearing, which allows visual images to be stored for about half a second and sounds for up to two seconds. Sensory memory enables television, which presents 30 still images per second, to convey the illusion of a single moving image. It also makes speech intelligible, because without it, by the end of each spoken word the hearer would have forgotten its beginning. *See also* sensory registers. *Cf.* long-term memory, short-term memory.

sensory registers subsystems of sensory memory (q.v.), such as (for vision) the iconic store and (for hearing) the echoic store generally assumed to exist separately for each sensory modality.

shaping a method of training animals and people to exhibit novel forms of behaviour by using a suitable schedule of reinforcement to reward successive approximations to the target behaviour, beginning with existing elements of the subject's behavioural repertoire.

short-term memory (STM) a memory store, also called working memory, consisting of a central executive, visuo-spatial sketchpad, and articulatory loop that is used for storing small amounts of information for periods of time ranging from a few seconds to a few minutes. It has a severely limited capacity of about seven or eight items of information, such as digits of a telephone number, and the information is rapidly forgotten unless it is refreshed by rehearsal, following which it may eventually be transferred to long-term memory (LTM) (q.v.). *See also* sensory memory.

Skinner box named after the American psychologist B. F. Skinner, a device for studying learning in animals, especially rats and pigeons, consisting of a box in which the animal can move a lever or peck a target to obtain reinforcement (q.v.), usually in the form of food.

social learning learning that occurs through observation of the behaviour of others, called models, together with imitation, and vicarious learning (q.v.).

social skills acquired proficiencies in verbal and non-verbal aspects of social interaction. *Cf.* cognitive skills, motor skills.

spontaneous recovery in conditioning, the reappearance of a response after its extinction (q.v.), following a period of rest.

stimulus (pl. stimuli) any objectively discernable event capable of evoking a response (q.v.) in an organism.

stimulus generalization in classical (Pavlovian) conditioning, the tendency to respond, after conditioning, to stimuli that resemble the conditioned stimulus; in operant conditioning (q.v.), the tendency to respond, after conditioning, to stimuli that were present during reinforcement.

subjects from the Latin *sub*, under, *jacere*, to throw, people or other organisms whose behaviour or mental experience is investigated in psychological research.

variable interval (VI) schedule *see under* schedules of reinforcement.
variable ratio (VR) schedule *see under* schedules of reinforcement.
vicarious learning from the Latin *vicarius*, substituted, learning that occurs through

110

the observation of others' behaviour and its consequences, also called observational learning. *See also* social learning.

working memory *see* short-term memory (STM).

Yerkes-Dodson law a psychological law named after its proposers stating that optimal performance on a variety of tasks occurs at intermediate levels of arousal (q.v.).

INDEX